An African-American Guide To Ethical Non-Monogamy

The How, Why and With Whom To Explore Your Expanding Love Styles

BY

TAYLOR K. SPARKS

An African-American Guide To Ethical Non-Monogamy

Copyright © 2023 Taylor K. Sparks

Contents

1. INTRODUCTION

Welcome to "An African-American Guide to Ethical Non-Monogamy" - a guide designed to help you navigate the complex world of love and relationships in a way that honors your cultural and personal values. As an African-American raised in the United States, you may have grown up with certain expectations and beliefs about sex and relationships that have been ingrained in you by society and religion. These stereotypes can limit our understanding of what is possible and prevent us from exploring our true desires.

In this guide, we will explore the various love styles under the umbrella of ethical non-monogamy, including open relationships, swinging, polygyny, polyandry, and polyamory. By examining these different approaches, we hope to help you discover which love style(s) resonate with you and which ones may not.

Our goal is not to convince you that one way of loving is better than another, but rather to help you explore the different options available to you in a way that is respectful and ethical. We will discuss ways to communicate openly and honestly with your partners, set boundaries that work for you, and take responsibility for managing your own emotions. I do not have all the answers to all of your questions. We are all coming into our awareness of ourselves, our needs and wants about relationships that makes us question if we are loving in a way that serves us best. This book is designed to be a foundation of information, not ALL of the information on ethical non-monogamy.

If you have ever been curious about ethical non-monogamy but weren't sure where to start, this guide is for you. It is a guide, not the bible, not the encyclopedia, but a guide to give you the base of where to start your journey with some facts about each of the love styles. If you have already begun your journey into ethical non-monogamy but are looking for answers on how to navigate your relationship(s), this guide is for you too. We hope that by reading this book, you will expand your understanding of love and relationships, challenge preconceived notions, and ultimately find the love and happiness that you deserve. So, let's dive in!

How It Started...

The question that seems to be asked of most couples when people find out they are ethically non-monogamous is: "Whose idea was it to open your relationship?" It was my idea twelve years into our twenty-five-year marriage to make the suggestion. We went to the famed Hedonism Resort in Negril, Jamaica, not with a swinger group, but ultimately met a lot of swingers, African-American swingers, and I had questions. I questioned everybody who would answer my questions. Why would you do this? How do you do this? Where do you do this? With whom do you do this? I was fascinated. But by the end of the week, we had decided that swinging wasn't our thing. After we came home, I was still curious about it all and Googled: "benefits of an open relationship" and found an article written from a husband's perspective. It seemed to make a lot of sense to me, so I asked my husband to read it. He, of course, thought I must be joking. I assured him that I was not and thought that having an open marriage would be better than swinging together. He wasn't keen on me being with other men, not because he didn't want to see me with other men, but rather he did not want to hear me with other men. My response was, "If you are with other women, I am going to be with men because I am not bisexual. So, either everybody is fucking or nobody is fucking." This is why being in an open marriage was better suited to us because we would do everything separately. So we first decided on our boundaries, and there were many:

- No family, friends, co-workers, or hotel staff.

- No one in the entire state of North Carolina.

- No spending the night.

- Always use condoms.

- Always let each other know where we were and with whom ahead of time.

- No falling in love.

- Give each other the space to talk about whatever it is regarding this agreement, good, bad, or ugly, and hold space for the person who is expressing their challenge or joy.

We both traveled for work out of the state, so that gave us opportunities to meet people for our 'excursions.' At the time, there was a popular website called *Black Swingers Club* where 99 percent of the members were swingers and African American. I decided that my first encounter would be with an ex-boyfriend from almost 20 years prior. We had always kept in touch over the years, and he had gotten divorced several years prior. So I called him up and said, "Hey, would you like to drive down to Virginia, and I will drive up, and we meet for lunch, and would you like to fuck me?" Without even breathing, he said, "Yep." So we made a date for about two weeks later. I asked him over lunch why he didn't ask what was happening in my marriage, and he said, "It really wasn't any of my business, and I thought you would tell me if you thought I should know." Good point. So that first experience, being with someone I knew and trusted, was great. Plus, I hadn't been with any other man in 12 years. It was quite the thrill! The second most asked question is: Why? People seem to think that you must be missing something from your relationship if you wish to explore outside of it or that there must be some 'issue.' Or perhaps one of you is a serial cheater and you think this will help (it will not, more later on that in the book). We had none of those issues. It really was a matter of wanting to do something different; it felt exciting to me, but more importantly, it felt 'right.' Meaning it felt like this was the type of relationship that I would have always had if I had known about it earlier in my life. My husband was just overjoyed at the thought of... new pussy. So we began. I was actually vetting the women on the site for him and setting up meet and greets with women in the states he was working, and he would decide to move forward with the women if there was a connection. We both would speak with her on the phone, and I could assure her that he was not cheating and I was not crazy, and to have a good time.

Being in an open relationship within the swinger community actually worked out well for us because we would meet couples, and sometimes there wouldn't be a four-way connection, and they could play separately. Or if there were singles at the resort, we could go our own way. We did that for almost two years before we finally met up with a couple that 'reeled' us in over the course of six months. We were invited to the wife's 30th birthday party in Atlantic City and were told that only a select few couples would be invited, and they knew that we didn't play in the same room, but everyone was going to be out in the open as they had rented a suite, and if we were not comfortable, we could go in one of the rooms. After two years, we thought, "Let's do it!" So off to Atlantic City we went. This couple had the whole suite laid out with sex toys, a sex swing, food, a full bar, and we all got goody bags with a $25 gambling chip. Once everyone arrived, we all went to dinner and gambled. When we got back, everyone stripped down to lingerie and the party began. That was our first orgy, and we were now...swinging.

Over the next few years, we had our twosomes, foursomes, and moresomes. We attended the annual Black Swingers Festival at Hedonism every year and started supporting their business. We then decided to produce our own events (Grown and Sexy Crew) so that we could go someplace other than Hedonism. Our first event was at Desire Resort in Cabo San Lucas. It was on our last day that we overlapped with an incoming group, Luxury Lifestyle Vacations Club. We met the owners and discovered that we lived only 20 minutes from each other in North Carolina. What were the odds? From that day to this day, our lives have been forever changed.

We began working with them as part of their customer service team. Our very first full ship takeover was on the Couples Cruise. We had no idea that the swinger community was big enough to privately charter an entire Royal Caribbean ship with more than 4,000 people! Luxury Lifestyle Vacations chartered a smaller but more luxurious cruise ship out of Athens, Greece, going to Istanbul, Turkey later that year. It was in our second year working with LLV that they hired me to develop a private label line of sensual massage oils and body washes for their company. At the time, I had an organic skincare company for elite athletes. I had developed a line of 16 head-to-toe products called Skin Care For Athletes Tri-Body Products. We sponsored marathons, triathlons, as well as triathletes and five Olympic athletes in both the winter and summer games. Once we launched the line, we realized we had no place to sell it, as I had a skincare for athletes brand and they had a travel agency. So, with a little love, money, and support from them, I launched OrganicLoven.com. I had also noticed that at most of the cruises, the vendors that were there were selling a lot of low-end toys and chemical-based products. With my background and certification in Holistic Aromatherapy, I started vetting organic intimate body products to carry on my site. I had been a Corporate Trainer for several years prior, training and coaching in the areas of communication, negotiation, management, leadership, customer service, and conflict resolution. I knew that humor was the best way to teach adults. So, instead of just standing behind a table to sell my products, I started developing seminars. My very first seminar was called "How To Make Good Pussy, Better." It was based on sexual health and wellness and an introduction to the newest and best sex toys on the market. The fun title stood out in a crowd of many seminars on the cruise ship, and it drove traffic to my site.

For the next 12 years, we traveled the world with Luxury Lifestyle Vacations, as well as hotel takeovers and other event producers such as Bliss Cruise, Naughty In Nawlins, Friction Parties, Kasidie Takeovers, Splash events, and Spicy Match events in Europe. We have cruised from Rome, Italy, to Barcelona, Spain; Stockholm, Sweden, to Amsterdam; Rio de Janeiro, Brazil, to Buenos Aires, Argentina, Alaska, and Paris River cruise. I was on the road more than he was as he still had a full-time job and I focused on growing the Organic Loven brand.

It was about seven years into our open relationship that I met a couple at Hedonism when I was there hosting a week for Luxury Lifestyle Vacations Club. It was this couple that introduced me to polyamory and kink. I was like the kid that put his back to the pool in the deep end, spread my arms, and fell all the way in. These... were my people! But... more on that later.

CHAPTER 2

Is Ethical Non-Monogamy a Choice or an Orientation?

P eople may choose ethical non-monogamy for a variety of reasons, such as a desire for more emotional or sexual diversity, a belief in the possibility of loving multiple people at the same time, or a rejection of traditional societal norms around monogamy.

There have been several debates on this subject. There are some who strongly believe that they have consciously chosen to be ethically non-monogamous (ENM). There are others who believe that their love style choice of ethical non-monogamy is an orientation, just as someone who is born homosexual or transgendered. Others still believe that only men were designed to be ethically non-monogamous, citing the many cultures where men are polygynous (one husband, more than one wife). Some even use biology as the reason, questioning why would men produce millions of sperm each day if not to impregnate multiple women? The real answer to that is because not many sperm make the journey to find an egg to fertilize. Some are strong swimmers; some don't have a good sense of direction. This is the reason why there are more sperm than are needed; it's a numbers game. Some are ENM by choice and only as a dating style. They date multiple people at the same time, letting all know that they are dating others. When they find one person who checks most of their boxes, they tend to settle into monogamy. While others have always been ENM and had no idea what it was called but knew there was a struggle to either feel content with just one person or had the feeling that there was more love to give and receive. So being ethically non-monogamous can be a choice for some and an orientation for others. Not right. Not wrong, just different.

CHAPTER 3

Ethics in Ethical Non-Monogamy

Ethics refers to a system of principles and values that guide behavior and decision-making. It involves distinguishing between right and wrong, good and bad, and just and unjust actions. Ethics can apply to a wide range of situations, including personal conduct, professional conduct, social policies, and more.

Practicing ethics in non-monogamous relationships requires clear communication, mutual respect, and a commitment to honesty and transparency. It requires you to:

1. Set clear boundaries: It's important to communicate your needs and boundaries with your partners and to respect theirs as well. This can include things like how often you see other partners, what types of physical intimacy you're comfortable with, and what types of relationships are "allowed" (e.g., casual vs. serious).

2. Communicate openly and honestly: Authentic honesty and transparency are key to building trust in non-monogamous relationships. Be upfront about your feelings and intentions, and make sure to communicate regularly with your partners.

3. Practice safe sex: Safe sex is important in any sexual relationship, but it's especially crucial in non-monogamous relationships where partners may be having sex with multiple people. Make sure to use condoms or other forms of protection and get tested regularly for sexually transmitted infections.

4. Be respectful of other partners: If your partner is seeing other people, it's important to be respectful of their relationships and boundaries, and they should be respectful of yours. Learn to manage your emotions and make sure to communicate openly and honestly with your partner about your feelings, especially uncomfortable emotions. It is better to have a difficult discussion when the feelings are just emerging, rather than waiting, as there is a good chance that unsettled resentment will form, which can lead to more unwanted emotions.

5. Handle conflicts with care: Conflicts are not inherently negative or positive; they simply exist. Conflicts can arise in any relationship, but they can feel especially challenging in non-monogamous relationships because you may be faced with situations that have never arisen in your monogamous relationships. For instance, your partner's sudden interest in salsa dancing, which leads them to attend salsa classes every Wednesday evening for 2.5 hours with a new partner. The conflict may not be solely a scheduling issue; it could involve internal emotions. It's important to handle conflicts with care and respect, and to communicate openly and honestly with all parties involved. Consider seeking the help of a coach if you are dealing with challenges that require guidance or a therapist if your emotions run deeper.

6. Practice self-care: non-monogamous relationships can be emotionally demanding for some and completely fulfilling for others. Therefore, it's important to prioritize your own needs and engage in self-care. This can involve setting aside time for yourself, such as going on a solo date when your partner is on a date. Additionally, practicing mindfulness or meditation and seeking support from friends, a coach, or a therapist, if necessary, can be beneficial. Remember that you and your partner are not attached at the hip, and it's perfectly okay to engage in activities that make you feel cared for and contribute to your overall well-being.

Nobody Belongs to Anybody

The phrase "nobody belongs to anybody" means that individuals have the right to make their own decisions and live their own lives without being owned or controlled by others. It suggests that people are not possessions or objects to be owned by others, and that everyone has the freedom to make choices about their own lives and relationships. Hence the quotes around the word "allowed" above. We may want or not want our partners to engage with certain people or to not "fall in love" because we are uncomfortable with it. It is totally okay to express that to your partner(s). But at the end of the day, their ultimate choice is their ultimate choice. Does it mean that they are not to take their partners into consideration? No, but we are not here to control or demand or even "allow" what emotions (relationships, sexual encounters, etc.) that our partners can have or not have. It can be a difficult pill to swallow when your partner may decide that they are wanting a deeper connection or more time with a new/different partner than what was originally thought or agreed upon. This does give you the opportunity to discuss and work through any emotions that you and they have and then decide where you go from there.

In a romantic context, this phrase could be interpreted as an assertion that no one person can fully possess another, and that true love involves respecting and supporting each other's autonomy and individuality.

Overall, "nobody belongs to anybody" is a reminder that we should respect each other's independence and agency and avoid trying to control or own others. This can be quite an adjustment coming from monogamy, where modern monogamy is just the opposite.

Boundaries vs Borders

Esther Perel, a psychotherapist, author, and speaker who specializes in the areas of relationships and sexuality, distinguishes between boundaries and borders by defining them as follows:

Boundaries are internal limits that we set for ourselves to protect our own needs, feelings, and values. These can include things like saying no when we don't want to do something, asking for what we need in a relationship, or setting aside time for self-care.

Borders are external limits that we set to protect ourselves from the outside world. These can include things like physical boundaries (such as fences or walls) or cultural boundaries (such as national borders or religious customs).

Perel suggests that while boundaries are important for healthy relationships, borders can sometimes create unnecessary conflict and separation. She argues that when we focus too much on borders, we can become overly defensive and mistrustful of others, which can lead to a breakdown in communication and intimacy.

A great analogy of hers that she used in her book, *The State of Affairs*, is that boundaries are more fluid like the shoreline on the beach. It moves as situations arise, and people have the authority over themselves to make the best decision for themselves at that time. We trust that they will also take their partner(s) into account, but ultimately the decision is what is best for them at that time.

When we set borders, masquerading as firm boundaries in our relationships (i.e., you can't spend the night, no kissing on the mouth, don't cum inside/don't have an orgasm, don't fall in love), it becomes like walls on either side of a canal that the boats pass through, immovable. There is nothing more than humans like to do than to cross borders. We don't want to rule our partner(s) and relationships as if they are two-year-olds who don't know how to cross the street because they are unaware of the dangers of getting hit by a car.

Instead, Perel suggests that we should aim to establish clear boundaries that protect our own needs and values while also remaining open and flexible enough to connect with others and navigate the complexities of our relationships. By finding this balance, we can create a sense of safety and trust that allows for deeper emotional connections and more fulfilling relationships.

CHAPTER 4

The History of Marriage

a. The History of Marriage

Marriage, as we know it today, has only been this way for the most recent two hundred years or less. Raising children together and coupling has been around for as long as humans have been on this earth. As our society started to expand about ten thousand years ago from being wandering hunters and gatherers to a more stationary life with the agricultural era, the first recorded event of marriage was during the Mesopotamian era between 2000-8000 B.C. In the beginning, marriage was a true contractual agreement where couples married to partner with someone, expand property, work the lands together, and have children to pass inheritance and land. Although it was strictly contractual, it doesn't mean that love, for some, didn't come over time. But love was the least of the focus on a good partnership.

Marriage had very little to do with love; it was about securing rights to land and making sure that the heirs were, in fact, the man's so that he could pass his land and possessions on to them. Of course, we all know that there was no way to be positive that the heirs were his, but if the woman said the child was his in marriage, it was his. Unless, of course, the child had such different features that there was no other way to know for sure.

As communities and cultures became more established, marriage became more institutionalized and civil, and some religious authorities started to add their own rules. As early as 2100 B.C., Mesopotamian laws were written with specific rules and laws about marriage and punishments if those laws were broken. These covered punishments for adultery and the legal status of any children that were born to slaves.

Many cultures allowed and agreed with marriages having more than one spouse, also known as polygamy. Husbands having more than one wife is called polygyny, and wives having more than one husband is called polyandry. It is still acceptable in about one-fourth of the world's cultures today.

But just because something was allowed didn't always make it possible. Most often, a man or woman could only marry as many wives as they could afford. So that meant that a man/woman of meager earnings could only have one or two spouses, whereas those who were wealthy could have multiple wives and/or concubines. In places like the Himalayas, women would marry and bear children of brothers so that the land could stay within the family instead of being divided into multiple households. 1

It may seem new to most of us, but same-sex unions have been discovered throughout history. Native Americans had those who were referred to as "Two-Spirit," which was/is a term used within some Indigenous communities, encompassing cultural, spiritual, sexual, and gender fluid identity. In Rome, both the emperors Nero and Elagabalus married men in public ceremonies, although it was banned in 342 A.D. There was an actual marriage recorded in 1061 between two men in a small chapel in Spain. There were also some places in both China and Sudan where people married "ghost" or deceased people to continue the family lineages or appease the spirits.

The one thing most of the marriages had in common during that time was that they were arranged, especially for those who had wealth and property. They did not let something as unstable as love get in the way of making the right connections and marital contracts. As stated above, the modern way we view marriage, with a focus on love and companionship, has only been around for the most recent 200 years. As industrialization, urbanization, and the middle class grew, more people became independent from their large extended families and focused on growing their own. As new ideas emerged, and people became more "enlightened," people started to focus on their own individual happiness. Some restrictions on divorce were lifted, and some people chose to marry at a later age. Marriage has always been shaped by society, and as societies change, so will marriage and how we view it.

b. The History of African-American Marriage

Most of us know about the slave trade, middle passage, and 400 years of slavery. Most know that many Black women were raped and bore their masters' children. Also, many of us know that, as property, African Americans were not allowed to marry during slavery, by law. There were some instances where "at the will of the master," slaves were allowed a ceremony but had to revise the vows of the civil unions, which, in part, stated, "you will be married until death or distance do you part."

The jumping-the-broom tradition, which many black Americans began to follow after it was shown on the television series Roots, was actually a tradition of the Celts and not originally from Africa, as many of us have been led to believe. Pre-Christian Roma and Celtic communities in the British Isles were notorious for jumping the broom to seal their wedding vows.[2]

Citing the research of Professor Dianne Stewart from her book *Black Women, Black Love: America's War On African-American Love*, we unearth the depths to which America has gone to keep black women and men from having fulfilling and loving relationships in a myriad of ways.

c. Relationships Torn Apart From Port to Port

Men and women were forcefully taken from their families before they arrived on the shores. In 1669, Hagar Blackmore, an 'Angolan' woman, appeared before the Middlesex County court in Massachusetts and recounted how she was snatched from her husband and the infant she was nursing. Her traumatic experience of being captured was made worse by the loss of love and life she had nurtured through her familial bonds. Blackmore's abduction and subsequent enslavement in America had severe consequences beyond the separation from her family. It permanently severed her connections to a potent kinship, which was the source of her social capital and personal significance. Marriage was the societal adhesive that bound her family and clan together. In Africa, regardless of whether one was polygynous, polyandrous, or monogamous, marriage was a crucial rite of passage that regulated social life, child-rearing, and elderly care. It provided guidelines for inheritance and served as the foundation through which one's lineage and clan thrived.[3]

During the African slave trade, many women who were abducted were typically aged between fifteen and thirty. Most of these women were already married and had children by the time they were taken. In some cases, both the husbands and wives were captured but ended up on different ships bound for different destinations, marking the beginning of the attack on Black love. As enslaved Africans were brought to the South, slave owners began to pair male and female slaves together to produce more offspring. Laws were established which declared that anyone born to a slave mother would also be a slave for their entire life, without any consideration for love or relationships.

Slave laws and customs were implemented to enforce and preserve the institution of slavery, but they also had a devastating impact on Black love and marriage. These laws not only made it difficult or impossible for couples living on separate plantations (called abroad marriages) to spend time together, but also deprived individuals of their freedom to choose their own partners and wedding rituals. The authority of slave owners superseded that of the enslaved, leaving spouses and children vulnerable to the horrors of the domestic slave trade, as well as physical, sexual, and mental abuse.

Women and girls were particularly subjected to the sexual advances of white individuals with access to their bodies, as they had nowhere to hide from the white gaze, the white penis, and stratification of beauty based on phenotype. The scale of sexual valuation within slavery made Black women of all phenotypes vulnerable to sexual exploitation. However, mixed-race individuals were often given preferential treatment by whites, creating a color-caste system that persisted for generations and continues to influence the Black marriage market today.

Since the beginning of colonial settlement, black enslaved women were highly regarded for their reproductive abilities. White slaveholders viewed their bodies as a means to fuel the growth of industries and accumulate wealth. With the expectation that natural increase would lead to an increase in the number of slaves they owned, these slaveholders developed both short- and long-term investment plans.

d. Revitalizing Black Matrimony and Household Establishment

After the Civil War ended, many African Americans were eager to become legal "citizens." The English patriarchy, which ruled in this country, did not grant women any rights of their own. They had no financial independence, and their husbands had legal authority over any property or contractual negotiations in which they may have owned or been involved. In 1865, Congress established the Bureau of Refugees, Freedmen, and Abandoned Lands to oversee relief for former slaves (and poor whites) as the South went on to rebuild after the war.

During this time, these agents traveled through the South, marrying black couples, and influencing them to embrace monogamy and the gender roles should be the same as the European standard, with the man as the head of the household, controlling all of the income and any contracts for labor. According to bureau agents, any deviation from monogamy in a marriage was seen as a threat to the sanctity of the institution and could potentially lead to women and children becoming reliant on the state for support. They gave no regard to previous marriages being polygynous, which many were arranged during slavery.

If a man had more than one wife, which many did, as they could have been loaned out for years at a time from one plantation to another and forced to 'mate' with another woman to produce more slaves for the plantation owner, he was forced to marry 'the one with the most children' so that they could receive their citizenship. The woman with fewer children was left to her own account, trying to find a way to support herself and her children. So, although patriarchal monogamy was supposed to protect the women and children, it did absolutely nothing for the many polygamous and arranged marriages that had taken place for many years during slavery, let alone the many women and children who were left with no one to support, provide, and protect them. States not only tried to force former slaves to marry, because when they did, the former slave owners could be released of any obligation to take care of their former property, but when former slaves refused to marry or did not do so in the appointed time, they were penalized.

The Freedman's Spelling-Book, published by the American Tract Society and distributed to post-enslaved persons around 1866, and the Christian Bible established Christian boundaries of moral behavior for husbands, wives, and children. The nuclear, patriarchal family within a heterosexual 'household' structure was the only legitimate basis for extended kinship networks. 5

e. History of African American Sexual Stereotypes

As noted in the "History of African-American Marriage" chapter, our relationships and how we were treated as less than human sent messages to and through us that still have roots within us today. During the slave and subsequent eras, several stereotypes about us and our sexuality became a sticking point. To a great degree, these stereotypes still exist today and contribute greatly to how we are seen and how we see each other. White women also had stereotypes, but the two are in opposite directions. White women have been and still are seen as pure, pious, delicate, moral, weak, domestic, virginal, and dependent, whereas black women represent hypersexual wantonness and are sexually aggressive.

These African-American stereotypes began during slavery and can be seen depicted today in our music videos, ads for food, liquor, and sports.

1. The "Jezebel" stereotype portrays African American women as promiscuous and sexually aggressive (Some of the roles portrayed by Pam Grier).

2. The "Mammy" stereotype depicts African American women as nurturing and subservient caretakers who prioritize the needs of white people (or others) over their own (Viola Davis in The Help).

3. The "Sapphire" stereotype portrays African American women as angry, hostile, and emasculating towards men, particularly Black men (Pam from the Martin TV series).

4. The "Strong Black Woman" stereotype portrays African American women as being able to endure and overcome any adversity without showing vulnerability or seeking help (Gina Torres, Suits).

African-American men have suffered and continue to suffer similar stereotypes.

The "Mandingo" stereotype portrays African American men as hypersexual and physically aggressive, with a supposed innate ability to satisfy white women sexually (Mandingo, 1975).

The "Brute" stereotype depicts African American men as violent, dangerous, and lacking in intelligence and self-control.

The "Thug" stereotype portrays African American men as involved in criminal activity and as being a threat to society (The beating of Rodney King, 1991).

The "Magical Negro" stereotype portrays African American men as having supernatural abilities or wisdom that can be used to benefit white people (Will Smith, The Legend of Bagger Vance).

The "Uncle Tom" stereotype portrays the African American who is subservient to white people and would sacrifice himself for his white master/employer (Samuel L. Jackson, Django Unchained).

CHAPTER 5

The History of Monogamy

T he history of monogamy is complex and varies greatly depending on cultural, religious, and societal beliefs. Monogamy refers to the practice of having only one spouse or partner at a time.

Historically, monogamy has been relatively rare among humans, with polygamy (having multiple spouses or partners) being much more common. In fact, many ancient societies, such as the Greeks, Romans, and Egyptians, practiced various forms of polygamy.

However, over time, monogamy began to gain popularity for various reasons. One of the most significant factors was the rise of Christianity, which promoted the idea of monogamous marriage as the ideal. In the Western world, this eventually led to the establishment of monogamous marriage as the legal and cultural norm.

Monogamy has also been advocated for by various social and political movements throughout history, including feminist and LGBTQ+ rights movements.

Today, monogamous relationships are widely accepted and considered the norm in many parts of the world, although there are still some cultures where polygamy is practiced.

It's important to note that while monogamy has become the norm in many societies, it is not inherently "better" or "more natural" than other forms of relationships. The important thing is for individuals to find the relationship structure that works best for them and their partners.

CHAPTER 6

Toxic Monogamy Explained

This is a term that has gained a lot of traction over the past few years, especially as ethical non-monogamy has received lots of exposure via social media and reality TV. But the question is, what is toxic monogamy and why and how did monogamy become labeled toxic? Toxic monogamy refers to societal norms and beliefs surrounding romantic relationships that can be harmful and restrictive. It is important to note that the term "toxic monogamy" does not imply that all monogamous relationships are toxic. Instead, it highlights certain negative aspects that can be present within some monogamous relationships or cultural expectations surrounding monogamy.

A few characteristics associated with toxic monogamy are as follows:

Possessiveness and jealousy: Toxic monogamy often promotes possessive behavior and extreme jealousy. Partners may feel the need to control or limit each other's actions, friendships, or interactions with others, leading to feelings of insecurity and mistrust.

Unhealthy expectations of exclusivity: Toxic monogamy may encourage the idea that one partner should be the sole source of emotional, physical, and sexual fulfillment for the other. This can place unrealistic burdens on individuals and may lead to feelings of inadequacy or guilt for seeking emotional support or connection outside the relationship. This can come up when you seek a "girls' night/weekend" or "boys' night/weekend" away from your partner.

Enforcing gender roles: Traditional toxic monogamous norms often reinforce rigid gender roles and expectations. These roles can limit personal expression, restrict individuality, and reinforce harmful stereotypes, such as men being emotionally stoic or women being submissive. Examples of this may be your male spouse not wanting to take care of the children or do the dishes.

Codependency: Toxic monogamy may foster codependent dynamics where individuals become overly reliant on their partners for self-worth, validation, and happiness. This can lead to an unhealthy imbalance of power and a lack of personal autonomy.

Relationship hierarchy: Toxic monogamy can perpetuate the idea that romantic relationships are inherently superior or more important than other types of relationships. This can devalue friendships, family relationships, or other forms of connection, creating an unhealthy hierarchy of relationships.

It is important to recognize that these characteristics can occur in any type of relationship, not just monogamous ones. The term "toxic monogamy" aims to shed light on the negative aspects of some societal expectations surrounding monogamy, encouraging healthier and more inclusive relationship practices. It is essential to foster open communication, respect for personal boundaries, and the recognition that each person's needs and desires may vary. Building a relationship based on trust, mutual respect, and individual growth can help counteract toxic monogamous norms and create a healthier, more fulfilling partnership.

CHAPTER 7

How Behavioral Epigenetics Affects Our Relationships

B ehavioral epigenetics is a field of study that investigates how environmental experiences and behaviors can affect gene expression through changes in the epigenome, which refers to chemical modifications that can turn genes "on" or "off" without changing the DNA sequence itself. This field seeks to understand the mechanisms through which social, behavioral, and environmental factors can shape an individual's gene expression patterns and how these changes may influence the risk of developing various physical and mental health conditions later in life. Some examples of environmental factors that have been studied in behavioral epigenetics include early-life stress, nutrition, drug use, and social interaction. By understanding how environmental factors can influence the epigenome, researchers may be able to identify novel targets for interventions and therapies aimed at preventing or treating various diseases and disorders.

Epigenetics can have an impact on your relationships in a variety of ways. Epigenetics refers to changes in gene expression that can occur without changes to the underlying DNA sequence. These changes can be influenced by a range of environmental factors, such as diet, stress, and social experiences, and can be passed down from generation to generation.

One way that epigenetics can impact your relationships is through the transmission of trauma. Studies have shown that traumatic experiences can cause changes in gene expression that can be passed down to offspring, potentially affecting their behavior and emotional regulation. This means that if one or both of your parents experienced trauma, you may be more likely to struggle with emotional regulation and may find it difficult to form healthy relationships.

Additionally, epigenetic changes can be influenced by social experiences. For example, studies have shown that social isolation and chronic stress can cause epigenetic changes that can lead to increased anxiety and depression. This can make it more difficult to form and maintain healthy relationships.

On the other hand, positive social experiences can also have a positive impact on epigenetic changes. For example, a supportive and nurturing environment can lead to changes in gene expression that promote emotional regulation and resilience. This can help you form and maintain healthy relationships.

Overall, while epigenetics can have an impact on your relationships, it is important to remember that it is just one of many factors that can influence your behavior and emotional regulation. By being aware of your own experiences and seeking out supportive environments and relationships, you can work to mitigate the effects of any negative epigenetic changes and foster positive ones.

Let's take a cinematic example of how epigenetics could affect future generations. When we look at the movie "12 Years a Slave," Lupita Nyongo's character was emotionally and physically abused and traumatized by her slave master, although he 'loved her' and could not relieve himself of the internal torment of loving this slave woman. So, he raped her almost daily, beat her for the slightest transgression, and she also had to contend with his jealous wife who also took out her anger and jealousy on her every chance she got. What might she tell her children (if she had them, especially with him) about how they would need to behave to survive slavery? What would she tell her children about relationships and love? What trauma would the children witness, even at an age too young to understand, about "relationships"? On the opposite of that experience was Alfrie Woodard's character, married to the man she loved, and we were led to believe he loved her, her 'master.' She did not work in the fields or within the house. She had slaves that catered to her every need. How would she transfer her emotions to her children (if she had them with him) about how to survive the environment of slavery based on her time in that era?

A great deal about how we "feel" about monogamy, relationships, and even love has been passed down to us externally by our environment, words, and actual demonstrations, as well as epigenetically from our ancestors who were enslaved for several generations. Behavioral epigenetics is how generational trauma is defined and explained. It can scientifically show us how much of what we have come to believe has been genetically and environmentally passed on—the good and the oh so ugly.

What is a belief? A belief is a thought that we continue to think based on what we have been told and experienced.

Your desire or willingness to be a part of an ethically non-monogamous union may or may not, in fact, be more from within than you have given prior thought to. It is quite possible that your ancestors were "poly" (polygyny, polyandry, polyamory), and this "feeling" of being more comfortable having more than one partner may have been passed on to you through epigenetics. One question recently posed by Alex Porter of the @PortahFamily (Instagram) was, "If you were raised with the choices of monogamy and nonmonogamy, instead of only monogamy as the default, would you have chosen monogamy?"

a. The Five Love Languages in Ethical Non-Monogamy

There are many ways to love. The Five Love Languages is a concept created by Dr. Gary Chapman in his book *The Five Love Languages: How to Express Heartfelt Commitment to Your Mate*. The idea is that people express and receive love in different ways, which can be categorized into five "love languages":

1. Words of Affirmation: This love language involves expressing love and appreciation through verbal affirmations, such as saying "I love you" or giving compliments.

2. Acts of Service: This love language involves expressing love through actions, such as doing chores or completing tasks for your partner.

3. Receiving Gifts: This love language involves expressing love through tangible gifts, such as flowers or jewelry.

4. Quality Time: This love language involves expressing love through spending time together, such as going on dates or engaging in activities together.

5. Physical Touch: This love language involves expressing love through physical touch, such as hugs, kisses, and holding hands.

What we tend to do is love people the way that we wish to love them, not in the manner that they wish to be loved. We usually love, parent, teach, and manage in the way that we loved, were parented, taught, or managed. So, if our parents put us to bed at 8 p.m., we will put our kids to bed at 8 p.m., without question, because it worked for us and we turned out okay, so it is okay if we do the same. Dr. Chapman suggests that identifying and understanding your partner's love language, as well as communicating your own love language, can improve the quality of your relationship and make your partner feel loved and appreciated.

So, how does this apply in ethical non-monogamy? The same. Understanding the way people wish to be loved can guide you into loving your different partners differently.

In addition, and specific to loving people, there are some distinct and some crossover characteristics in the "love styles" under the umbrella of ethical non-monogamy (ENM). Here we will cover each of these styles, how they function, and the mindset of those who practice these styles. Keep in mind that there will always be some characteristics that overlap with others. This is to give you some foundation to review and/or start, but not to put you in a box. As you enter and move through ethical non-monogamy, you will see that everyone has put their own little "twist" on it. Being aligned within yourself and within the relationship(s) that you have is what is most important. If you and they agree with how you all will have and explore your relationship(s), it is not a matter of right or wrong...just different.

CHAPTER 8

The Ethical Non-Monogamous Love Styles

L ove...is a decision. We choose to love our partners. The best thing about being at the top of the food chain is that we have choices! Most others in the animal kingdom operate solely on instinct. Meaning that if a female is in heat just once a year, and if the male does not mate with her during that time frame, he must wait until next year. There are only a few other species that have sex just for the pleasure of having sex: humans, bonobos, dolphins, lions, apes, macaques, chimpanzees, and male sea otters. The rest are on the clock. So, knowing that you have chosen to love a person, you can also choose to love them in the manner that they wish to be loved, as well as express how you wish to be loved because they chose you.

CHAPTER 9

Defining "Open"

The definition of an open relationship is one in which the partners/spouses have agreed to having sex with others outside of their own relationship. This type of relationship focuses more on sexual encounters and less on romantic encounters that may lead to future relationships. Most open relationships are sex-based, but there may be times when it is just a dinner date.

What It Is

This type of relationship can be applied and useful in many relationship styles. It can allow one or both partners with widely varying libidos and/or sexual preferences the opportunity to have those differences fulfilled. This can take the "pressure" off their partner to satisfy those needs, wants, or desires that they have no interest in or that could be challenging to maintain.

What It Isn't

This is not a permission slip to cheat (see the definition of cheating in ENM) and break any boundaries that you and your partner(s) have set up. It does not give you the freedom to not consider your partner's sexual health and emotions.

How It Functions

In some relationships, partners have agreed to a "don't ask, don't tell" arrangement. In this situation, the partners may agree that they will each have casual sex with others, or only one of the partners will, but not disclose specific information. Open relationships have their own set of negotiated boundaries and should be explicitly discussed. It may seem like some things are "just the way you do it," but making assumptions about how you want to be open versus how they want to be open can lead to unnecessary conflict. Safe sex is a must – the use of barriers (condoms, dental dams, regular STI testing and results). But one of the partners may decide that condoms, etc., are not always necessary.

a. Everyone may not have the same "risk" threshold. But it does happen where one partner does not feel the need or want to use barriers. I know what you are thinking... Who would agree to have unprotected sex in these times? This is why having these hard discussions is so important, ahead of time, and not assuming that you are thinking and wanting the same things. This can have a very serious impact on your relationship if this discussion is not had at the outset of opening your relationship, as opposed to looking over and seeing your partner engaged without using or having one used with them. How do you negotiate this? Discussing your own risk threshold and how this will affect your mindset within the relationship is most important. This is not the time to decide to imply that your beloved is uncaring (or worse) because they have chosen it unnecessary. b. Sexual boundaries. Are we having sex only with strangers? Only when out of town on business? Will they want to see the person again or on a regular basis (i.e., fuck buddies)? What types of sex are they having...penetrative, same-sex, oral, kissing, anal? Will there be BDSM involved in this open arrangement?

b. Emotional boundaries versus borders. As noted, Esther Perel stated in her book The State of Affairs: "Whereas borders are constructed as unquestionably right...boundaries are what is right at the time, for the particular people involved in a particular situation. Whereas borders claim the unquestionable and rigid authority of law, boundaries have a fluidity, an openness to change, more a riverbank, less a stone canal. Borders demand respect, boundaries invite it. Borders divide desirables from undesirables, boundaries respect the diversity of desires."7

This can be challenging because we can ask that our partners not get emotionally involved with someone, but we are also not trying to control our partners and their emotions. We are humans; we have emotions. You will need to have some sort of emotion just to like the person enough to have sex with them. So, asking that your partner not have any emotions is unrealistic. You may request that if your partner begins to feel stronger emotions, they let you know. If/when they do, now what do you do with that information? You can discuss what more they want to do with that person. What does it mean for your relationship? Or do you just want to know how it is all going? Or do you now want to meet that person? Your partner having more emotions for another person does not take away the emotions they have for you. Having the discussion is most important because you don't want to police a grown person.

a. **Scheduling check-ins.** Check-ins are not to be masked as another way to try to control your partner. Someone may request a physical check-in regarding arriving at their destination safely and/or on their way home. Emotional check-ins can be scheduled to have a safe space to process your emotions during the beginning of opening your relationship. You can also schedule an emotional check-in every few months or once a year after you have had some experiences that need to be sorted out or boundaries, they/you want to renegotiate.

b. **Authentic Honesty** – Being authentically honest can be a challenge for some of us, especially when coming from monogamy. In monogamy, we can sometimes believe it's best not to bring up feelings or incidents that may emotionally hurt or even anger our partners. So, we keep things to ourselves, like the fact that the condom broke during sex and bodily fluids were exchanged. Or that you really want to remove the "no spending the night" boundary because you truly do want to spend the night. Understanding that your partner may have insecurities or fear or even jealousy gives you the opportunity to express and explore these emotions. They are not delicate flowers; they will not fall to the floor in a heap when you tell the truth. Give yourself the opportunity to say how you are really feeling so that you all can get through whatever emotions may come up. It will make your relationship stronger and expose areas where you both need to work on. When you do not fully disclose whatever has happened or how you are feeling, and you are 'found out,' the partner can have feelings of betrayal and be even more hurt than if you had just told the truth from the beginning. Trust me, in ENM, honesty really is the best and most wanted emotion.

c. **Current Relationship Consideration** - Keep your current relationship in mind. Take your partner and their feelings into consideration. If you have been in a relationship for some time or a long time, the excitement of a new pussy or dick and your heart will keep your mind racing with what is called N.R.E. - new relationship energy. New Relationship Energy is just what it sounds like. Although you may not be in a 'relationship' with this new person, the thought of being 'free' to explore your desires can keep you out past whatever time frame you have set or start to miss dates and check-ins with your current partner. It can even make you 'move your boundaries' over just a bit because of the thrill of this new frontier. So as an adult, check yourself. Your partner should not have to come behind you and scold you like a 6-year-old who forgot to pick up the toys they took out of the box and left all over the kitchen floor. Remember, you have decided to explore an open relationship together, even if only one of you is currently or ever going to be having sexual encounters outside of your relationship.

Why Mindset

Why do you want to open your relationship? That is the discussion you must have with yourself and your partner(s) before stepping outside of your relationship. It may feel like a very difficult discussion to broach, but trying to back into it from the position of infidelity will make it even more difficult, as you have already broken the trust. It's a "you can't get there from here" scenario. Yes, it can be done, but it will be much more difficult because of previous deceit and/or betrayal.

Open relationships give you an opportunity to explore your sexual desires, sexual proclivities, and balance out significant differences in libidos. This opportunity comes without having to damage the current relationship by cheating or betraying your partner, as you enter into this agreement together. As with all ethical non-monogamous relationships, having an open mind, being responsible, and being in control of your own emotions is going to assist you in having success in any of these relationship styles.

Open relationships can be easier for some, as you can choose to "not know" any details, thereby sparing yourself from some emotional turmoil...like whether the other person is sexier, has a better body, earns more, or is kinkier. Keeping your partners' sexual encounters at arm's length doesn't require a lot of input from you. Discuss what needs to be discussed, set the boundaries, and leave the rest outside the door.

A Common Question: Why am I not enough? I'm putting this question early in the book because it comes up in every type of ENM love style, so let's address it here and now. This is an often-asked question by the partner wanting to open the relationship to the partner being asked to participate in an ENM relationship. I am not here to tell you how to answer the question. It could be a question that never comes up. For those who have been faced with that question, some of the answers have been: You are enough. I want more and/or different (sex, kink, experiences, etc.), and me wanting that does not take anything away from who you are and what you offer to me. Another answer: I believe this can relieve the pressure that we put on each other to give more than we are able or to ask for less than we want from each other. I have personally referred to "not being a pie," meaning that there are only so many slices in the pan, and once all those slices are given out, there isn't any left. Love...is infinite. Anyone with more than one child can tell you the precise moment their love expanded when the second or third child was born. No, love for your children is not different from love for your partner or your mother or your father. Love is...love. It expands, and we cannot keep it from expanding because we demand the full attention of a partner. Love may be infinite, but time is not. We can only love as many people as we have time for and still meet our needs and the needs of our partners, families, etc. Society and marketing (one true love, soul mate, etc.) have implied that we require another to "complete" us. But if you did not know, you were complete when you entered the relationship, and you will still be complete if or when you decide to open it or leave it.

Examples

An example of how one may operate in an open relationship may include:

a. They may state they are going on a *"date"* to let their partner know they are meeting up with someone, usually for the purpose of sex, but it could be just dinner. But they may not tell them the name, or sex of the other person. They may only state how long they will be out on the date.

b. For others, they may have agreed to give more information, about whom they will be with and where they will be located. How long the date will last, a few hours or overnight.

It is up to the partners to decide what information is wanted for this Open love style. No one else can determine what is the right way if you are **both** in agreement. In agreement is the operative phrase.

CHAPTER 10

Defining "Swinging (aka The Lifestyle)"

T he definition of swinging or being in the lifestyle is a person or persons that consensually engage in sex with other individuals, couples or more. Swingers can be a couple or a single individual, male or female, heterosexual, bi-sexual, gay, pan sexual, etc.

What It Is

Most people who identify as swingers are physically non-monogamous and emotionally monogamous. It is not their intention to seek an emotional bond or engage in an on-going romantic relationship with the person or people that they have sex with, although it can/does happen on occasion. Many people who swing are couples, but there are a number of single women. Single women are most desired and welcomed in the lifestyle due to a high number of bi-curious/bi-sexual women and the female/male/female fantasy wanting to be fulfilled. Single bi-sexual women are called 'unicorns' because they are so rare to find in the lifestyle. As soon as someone finds a 'unicorn', they marry her! There are also single women who are not bi-sexual, and they are not considered 'unicorns', unicorns are single bi-sexual women. More below on the differences and how they fit in within the lifestyle.

It is not a requirement to be in a relationship to be a swinger. Most couples prefer to swing with other couples because it is their belief that if a man/woman swap with each other, it is an even exchange. It is usually a couple in a committed relationship and the belief is that a person who cares for their own partner's sexual well-being, that that care will transfer over to the partner that they are swapping with. There is also the belief that with everyone in committed relationships there is less likely a chance to become more heavily involved because when the sex is over, everyone goes back to the respective partners. That is mostly true. Has it ever happened that opposite partners fall for each other? Yes, of course, and it has nothing to do with being in the lifestyle. We will cover these 'emotional risks' in the chapter on emotions.

What It Isn't

This is (again) not a permission slip to cheat (see the definition of cheating in ENM) and break any boundaries that you and your partner(s) have set up. It does not give you the freedom to not consider your partner's sexual health and emotions. If you have agreed to always use barriers, then suddenly deciding to not use barriers without any communication with your partner (before, during, or after) can be considered unethical, cheating, or a broken boundary. It will depend on what has been established within your relationship. It is not a 'free for all'. Meaning, when invited to a lifestyle party, club, resort, hotel takeover, you should not come with the expectation(s) that anyone and/or everyone that you feel a connection will feel the same about you. Even though there may be many people at the event open to having sex with others, it doesn't mean that you will be invited to indulge. These events are designed for people to get to meet each other for a 'possible' connection, and if it happens, there is a safe space to do it. It does not mean that it will happen each time you attend. Think about how long it took for you to find your current partner. Why would you think that you could walk into a party, and someone would be ready to lay down naked with you just because you showed an hour's worth of interest? If you are single/unattached within the lifestyle, these events are not a smorgasbord. Yes, there are many couples seeking a 'third', but it doesn't mean that you are the chosen one. Just like any other dating scene, seek to make acquaintances first.

How it Functions

Like open relationships, swinging gives you an opportunity to explore your sexual desires, sexual proclivities, desire for sexual variety, or balance out large differences in libidos. Swinging is a form of recreational social sex between consenting adults, most commonly consisting of male/female couples meeting other male/female couples for sex and/or ongoing intimate friendships. Our sexual needs, wants, and desires change as we age and as the relationship ages. Humans never stop evolving, and desire hardly ever wanes. It can be suppressed but doesn't entirely go away.

Building upon what we learned in how open relationships function, most all of those can be applied to swinger relationships. Here are some additional functions within the swinger community, and there really isn't a wrong or right way, just different ways. You and your partner will decide what works best for you, and that will be the best way to navigate the lifestyle.

Swinger Styles

Soft Swap

Soft swap typically involves couples deciding to engage in almost every type of intimate play, except for genital penetration. That could include kissing, hugging, flirting, touching of genitals, and even oral sex. There are many reasons why a couple may choose soft swap. Some of them could include:

1. New to swinging and not yet comfortable with penetrative sex with others.

2. Consider penetration 'too intimate'.

3. One of the partners is not ready for penetrative sex.

4. No desire to indulge in penetrative sex with others.

Note: There is no 'requirement' or need to move/elevate from soft swap to full swap. I have met many couples that have been soft-swap for more than 10 years. You will find others that enjoy what you enjoy, and you shouldn't let anyone pressure you into doing any more than you want or feel comfortable doing. You are no less a swinger because you choose to only soft swap.

Full Swap

As soft swap includes almost everything other than penetrative sex, full swap includes most everything, including penetrative sex! I say "most" and not "all" because there are couples who full swap that may not include kissing, anal, or oral sex. Yes, it's still a full swap, just with exceptions. There are many reasons why a couple may decide to choose full swap. Some of them include:

1. New to swinging and want the full experience right from the beginning.

2. Enjoy watching their partner or being watched by their partner indulging in sex with others.

3. It's a long-time fantasy, and they never tire of seeing it.

4. They and/or their partners enjoy the sexual variety. Their high libido can be satiated.

One Partner Plays

In this relationship, one partner has chosen not to participate in soft or full swap sexual activity. It is not uncommon and can be this way for different reasons. Some reasons why they have chosen why only one partner plays:

1. One of the partners is bisexual and only wants to play with others of their same sex.

2. One partner is solely involved in the lifestyle to play with others to satisfy their high libido. Their partner only wishes to indulge their partner.

3. One partner is a "voyeur" and only wants to see their partner being ravished.

4. Just because one partner doesn't want to have sex with you or anyone else, doesn't mean they don't still desire sex and/or intimacy.

5. You are not attached at the hip.

Why Mindset

Why would you want to move in the direction of swinging, either from an open relationship or directly from an ethically monogamous relationship? For some, the thought of embarking on this new sexual journey with your partner is more exciting than doing it without them. It becomes the secret life that the two of you live, share, and explore together. Being able to stand around "vanilla" couples and giggle at the thought that just the previous weekend you were at a resort with a group of swingers indulging in sex with others. You may both have fantasies of being watched or watching others have sex. You may have a fantasy to see your partner with another person of the opposite or same sex, or the fantasy may be theirs, to have you watch them.

It's also possible you are seeking a way to level out the differences in libido, meaning one person may have a very high libido and their partner a much lower libido. This gives the one with the higher libido an opportunity to satisfy their higher need without having to pressure their partner for more sex. It also relinquishes the partner with the lower libido from feeling the need to feel guilty for doing more than they are willing or capable of in satisfying their partner. I have heard hundreds of reasons why people have decided to become involved within the lifestyle. There is no one answer as to why you and/or your partner have decided to explore or expand. The bottom line will always be: does it feel right for you and them? If so, that is all that matters.

Examples of Swinger Identities

The Single Man In The Lifestyle

There are many single men who identify as 'swingers'. It may seem, at first glance, that single men cannot be 'swingers' and that they are just single guys having lots of sex with single women and couples. But single *successful* male swingers are very different than regular single men in today's society. Those differences include, being invited to swing parties, being allowed special nights at some swing clubs, being invited to accompany couples to events and swing parties. Single male swingers have a much higher success rate of indulging in casual sex on a weekly basis than your average single man, unless that man is in a high-profile profession, like professional sports or entertainment and even they may not compete with the number of sexual encounters a successful single swinger male can have over a weekend. Several successful single swinger males that I know have easily had 20 or more encounters and/or women over a weekend at an event. Most single men will be lucky to have 3 or even 5 on any given weekend. The opportunities are just not there for your average single guy.

A single male's approach to a couple should entail making acquaintances with the husband or boyfriend and/or then the wife. It is a sign of respect for their relationship. Even if the wife approaches a single male first, noting her desires, the well-informed single man knows that it is usually the husband that gives the ok as to whether another man can indulge his wife. Even if the wife is the one that makes the final decision, it is in his best interest to engage the husband/boyfriend to discuss what their boundaries are, how they 'play', if there are time limits, etc. Asking her what it is that she desires most and discussing who and if there are any boundaries that the single man should know about. It is to his advantage to discuss how long he's been in the lifestyle, parties, and places he's been, other couples he knows who can vouch for him. This will not only give him better chances of having the sexual encounter(s) he desires but to have him be invited to many future 'couples only' parties/events. If he does have the opportunity to indulge the wife and he wishes to continue to stay in touch, that too is a question that should be proposed to both partners. Although they are separate individuals, the relationship is one entity, so treat it as such by getting clarification along the way. Does the husband/boyfriend expect you to always go through him regarding communication with the wife/girlfriend? Can she meet with you alone? If yes, what are the boundaries, sexual expectations, time restrictions, etc.? Even though this is primarily a sexual encounter, the more respect you show the couple and her, the more likely you will be invited for another encounter.

Having great communication skills, an easy disposition, confidence in oneself, good sexual performance, great hygiene, proof of regular STI testing and respect for all involved…couples and singles alike, will keep a single man active in the lifestyle for as long as he desires. And like unicorns, most single men in the lifestyle enjoy being single. It doesn't mean that they are not open to having a relationship or relationships.

Some of the reasons that single men may not have great success in the swinger community at certain times (some clubs, events, or parties) include:

1. Insecurities of the partnered men (husband/boyfriend fears the single man may be in better shape, have a bigger penis, or more money).

2. Female partner of the couple may only be interested in 'playing' (having sex) with other women and only desires sex with her male partner.

3. Not treating the woman in a couple with the level of respect required by her and her partner, resulting in no longer indulging with single men.

4. Not having the social and/or communication skills to navigate the swinger community of couples. Poor sexual performance and/or personal hygiene are also factors. Yes, performance counts!

5. Inability to handle the performance.

The Single Woman in the Lifestyle (not the Unicorn)

Single women who are involved in the lifestyle have a much easier go at it than single men. Mostly because, who doesn't like a highly sexual woman at the sex party? They do, however, require the same level of requirements as single men when seeking to interact with a couple. They may get some leeway because they are women, but they too can quickly be uninvited to events, especially if drama comes a-calling.

To navigate the swinger community as a single woman, the first and most important communication must be with the wife/girlfriend of the man she may be attracted to or vice versa. It is important to treat the couple as one entity, and in this case, female-to-female communication is crucial. Sometimes, and I'm making a big generalization here, when a man is on the hunt for new partners, he will say just about anything to get it. It is better for the woman to wait and get a clear okay from his female partner than believe anything that comes out of his mouth.

The single female should find out how long the couple has been involved, how long they have been active in the lifestyle, what they like about it or not, be complementary to his partner, find out whose idea it was to become involved in the lifestyle. The questions from woman to woman are more personal because women bond differently. Find out how they play, what is and isn't acceptable, and take a little more time to get to know her, not quite ignoring him, but she will give the final okay.

It is common knowledge that women 'run' the lifestyle. It is the women who determine who gets and doesn't get pussy. Remember that this community is mostly composed of couples. Most men learn very early on that they have an advantage over their monogamous friends because their partners 'allow' them to engage sexually with other women (or men in bisexual relationships), even if it is only on one cruise a year, and she can shut it down at any time—and she will, if necessary. Are there men who are more dominant in their relationships within the lifestyle and control how they interact? Yes.

For the single woman, it is best to keep in mind how she would want to be treated if she were the one with the partner that another woman was pursuing. Letting the couples know about her own great experiences, her sexual health and STI status with regards to how often she is tested, events she has been to, couples she has played with that can vouch for her, and if she has a single male that could also join in on the fun if wanted or required. Sometimes couples will only play with other "couples" because they don't want to be separated or have one partner not be involved, especially if no one is bisexual (man or woman). They do not always care that the "couple" is romantically involved or not, just that the two of them know how to sexually navigate a couple. In the lifestyle, "fuck buddies" can take on a different meaning altogether because they may travel and sleep together but never actually have sex with each other, just the couples. They are, in a sense, each other's wing person.

There are single women who are "bi-comfortable," meaning that although they do not consider themselves bisexual, they may indulge in kissing or breast play with another woman or even be okay with a woman giving her oral sex. I used to say that I was "bi-party" because every now and again, I'd be at a swinger party, getting fucked from behind, and suddenly there would be pussy in my face. It was usually the woman of the man who was fucking me, and since I didn't want to stop the action, my thought was... I guess I'm eating pussy tonight. #KeepThePartyGoing

The Unicorn (single, bisexual female swinger) The difference between a single woman and the elusive unicorn is that firstly, she is bisexual, and secondly, she really does believe that she is somewhat of a "conduit" between the male and female couple. They are called "unicorns" because they are so hard to find, and everyone wants one. When a single guy happens upon one, he usually marries her! Successful unicorns in the lifestyle truly enjoy and, dare I say, love couples. They enjoy not only loving both partners but also helping the couple's bond become even closer. They love demonstrating to each partner new and exciting ways to please each other. They enjoy befriending them both and pleasing them both. Many times, they can end up being a couple's pseudo-therapist as they have spent time with each of them alone and together. In addition, as a unicorn, she gets twice the love, sex, friendship, trips, gifts, and party invites. She is sexually free, free in spirit, sure of herself, and answers to no one.

The Manicorn (single, straight male swinger) The Urban Dictionary defines a Manicorn as a mythical male creature who is successful (read: pursuing his passion and can pay his electric bills/rent), funny, chivalrous, masculine (read: not chauvinistic), adventurous, artistic (read: not suicidal). What's the difference between him and a single male swinger? Not much, other than he could be way more outgoing, bordering on flamboyant and loving to be the center of attention. He enjoys being the center of attention, flirting, and complimenting all of the women. He is often invited as he makes all the ladies feel wanted, even if he himself doesn't want them.

The Bull (single, straight or bi male swinger)

The Bull is a sexually dominant male who, for fun or (financial gain), cuckolds and humiliates husbands while sexually servicing their wives. He has sex with women who are in committed relationships with other men. In some cases, the interaction between the bull and the woman is meant to humiliate the woman's partner (a cuckold) by making him feel inferior to the bull. In other cases, like when a bull has sex with a vixen or a hotwife, there is no humiliation aspect involved. The woman's partner both knows about and encourages her sexual exploration with her bull.

One other less known but practiced form of ethical non-monogamy

Monogamish

The term "monogamish", coined by podcaster Dan Savage, refers to a relationship style that allows for some degree of sexual or romantic exploration outside of the primary partnership, while still maintaining a core commitment to each other. The exact parameters of a monogamish relationship can vary from couple to couple and can include anything from occasional flirting with other people to full-fledged sexual relationships with outside partners.

In a monogamish relationship, communication and honesty are key. Both partners need to be open and transparent about their desires, boundaries, and any experiences they have with outside partners. It's also important to establish clear rules and agreements about what is and isn't allowed, and to revisit these agreements regularly to make sure both partners are still comfortable and on the same page.

Some people find that a monogamish relationship allows them to explore their sexuality or emotional connections in a way that feels fulfilling and authentic, while still maintaining the security and intimacy of a committed partnership. However, it's not for everyone, and it's important to approach this style of relationship with honesty, respect, and a willingness to adapt and communicate as needed.

CHAPTER 11

Defining Polygamy

Polygamy is the practice of having more than one spouse at the same time. It is a form of marriage in which a person is allowed to have multiple spouses simultaneously. Polygamy can take various forms, including polygyny (a man having multiple wives), polyandry (a woman having multiple husbands), or group marriage (several people, regardless of gender, being married to each other). Polygamy is practiced in various cultures and religions around the world, although it is illegal in many countries.

CHAPTER 12

Defining "Polygyny"

P olygyny is the practice of having multiple wives, and it has taken different forms throughout history and across cultures. Traditional polygyny refers to the practice of having multiple wives within a traditional, usually patriarchal, social and cultural context. In traditional polygyny, a man's ability to take multiple wives is often seen as a sign of wealth, status, and power, and it is often linked to religion, custom, or tradition.

Modern polygyny, on the other hand, refers to the practice of having multiple wives in a contemporary context, where it may be influenced by factors such as individual choice, personal preference, and social and economic factors. Unlike traditional polygyny, modern polygyny may not be tied to religion or tradition, and it may be seen as a personal lifestyle choice.

What It Is

Polygyny is marriage-based, meaning that there is a legal marriage between the husband and one wife. Depending on the country and its laws, it may be legal to marry more than one woman. For other countries, there is a commitment ceremony that is considered, in the eyes of the couple, a commitment of marriage, and both or more women are recognized as wives of the husband. Most modern and traditional people who practice polygyny are family-focused. It does not always have a religious foundation (e.g., Muslim, Mormon). In traditional polygyny, women may have limited autonomy and power, and their value may be tied to their ability to bear children and maintain the household. In modern polygyny, women have more agency and can negotiate the terms of their relationship with their husband, but their husband is still the leader of the family, finances, and child-rearing.

In many countries, traditional polygyny is illegal, and it is seen as a violation of women's rights. However, in some countries, such as Saudi Arabia, traditional polygyny is legal, and it is practiced within the bounds of the law. In contrast, modern polygyny may be legal in some countries, but it may not be recognized by the law or accepted by society.

What It Isn't

It is not a sex-based love style. Of course, there is sex as most of the polygynous marriages have children, and not to say that sex isn't important. Sex is important in most all relationships, regardless of love styles. There must be a legal marriage, not just a relationship(s) with partners that may or may not be living together. If there is no marriage with at least one of the wives, then you are in a polyamorous relationship with more than one woman. There are many social media sites that promote their sexual references of the two women being sexually involved with each other, which, again, would be considered polyamorous (see polyamorous definition) rather than polygamous.

How It Functions

Polygyny, like all ethically non-monogamous love styles, requires a high level of maturity, security in oneself, honest and authentic communication skills, patience, and consideration. I emphasize this point because often both (or more) wives are living either under the same roof or in close proximity to their co-wives. A polygynous marriage may initially be monogamous, even if there are plans to bring on an additional wife. It could be early in the marriage or later when the husband approaches his wife about wanting to "marry" another wife. Overall, the practice of polygyny has evolved over time, and its form and meaning have changed depending on the cultural, social, and historical context. While traditional polygyny may still be practiced in some parts of the world, modern polygyny is becoming more common, raising new questions and challenges for individuals, families, and societies.

Mindset

Using the steps from Coach Nazir from the Outstanding Personal Relationships YouTube channel and their coaching on polygamy education, here is a checklist to review. He suggests that a husband ask himself the following questions before discussing (not asking permission) the idea of wanting to enter polygamy with his wife.

1. Self-evaluation – Rate yourself and your past achievements as a husband. Are you fulfilling the role as a husband? Are you providing, protecting, and building instead of destroying? Are you being proactive and intentional versus being careless? Being a "good husband" is demonstrable.

2. Have you considered the ramifications of bringing this up to her? Are you going to practice polygyny or not practice it? What if your wife is totally against it and threatens to leave and/or take the kids? Will you be steadfast or break down and say, "never mind"? Then, how will you deal with the resentment that builds up within yourself because you have allowed someone else to

make the decision as the leader of your household? It may or may not, but it is a question to ask yourself.

3. Have you ever discussed polygyny with her in the past? Saw something on TV or one of the polygyny coaches' videos? Maybe at the time you did discuss it, you were not ready or even sure it was something that you wanted to do. Or the topic became heated, and you left it alone.

4. Have you ever breached her trust, and there was another woman involved? If you have, are you going to trigger some very strong emotions? Have you worked through that already?

5. Does she have either a growth or a limited mindset? This also goes for you. Does she take accountability for what she has done, or is she always placing blame?

6. What is your communication style, and what is hers? Do you both have effective listening skills? Communication is both talking and listening. Is one of you more of a speaker or listener?

7. Does she have any traumas that can be triggered? Many of us do not get therapy or the personal development that is needed. Has she had therapy, if needed? How well do you know your wife?

8. Do you know your personality types? Taking personality assessments such as Myers Briggs or DISC can assist you in seeing how each of you acts, interacts, and reacts with each other.

Example

One example of polygyny today, in both the traditional religious-based and the more modern outlook, is Coach Nazir with his two wives, Coach Fatimah and Coach Nyla. They are the founders of Outstanding Personal Relationships and Polygamy Bootcamp, and they are practicing Muslims in the US. Nazir was married to Fatimah for 15 years before he decided to practice polygyny and take on an additional wife, Coach Nyla. The three of them have twelve children together, and one of their businesses involves coaching men and women on how to enter polygyny and have a successful polygynous relationship. They have several videos, books, and courses on polygyny, communication skills, and experiences. Their marriage is religious based but offers a modern outlook on how to navigate this style of relationship.

Here are some examples of the benefits of polygynous relationships:

1. Companionship: Having multiple partners can provide companionship and love to all members.

2. Shared responsibilities: Women are still the main providers of children and household chores. Having multiple partners lifts the burden and can make the day-to-day responsibility of running a household easier.

3. Stronger family unit: In most polygamous relationships, having additional parental units and extended family members can provide more emotional and social support to children and parents, creating a great sense of connection and community.

4. Financial stability: Having more partners who earn and collectively contribute to the household and the growth of the family offers more financial stability and opportunities for wealth building.

5. Diverse perspectives: Different partners bring different thought processes, outlooks, and experiences to the relationship. These different perspectives offer each member an opportunity for growth.

CHAPTER 12

Defining "Polyandry"

P olyandry is a form of marriage and/or partnership in which a woman has multiple husbands at the same time. It is the opposite of polygyny, which is a form of marriage in which a man has multiple wives. Polyandry can take different forms, including fraternal polyandry, where a group of brothers marry the same woman, or non-fraternal polyandry, where unrelated men marry the same woman. Polyandry is a rare form of marriage and is mostly found in some traditional societies in parts of Asia, Africa, and South America. One country where polyandry is legal and practiced is Nepal, a landlocked country in South Asia. Polyandry is a traditional practice among certain ethnic groups in the mountainous regions of Nepal, such as the Sherpas and Tamangs. In these communities, brothers will often share a wife to keep the family property intact and avoid dividing it among multiple heirs.

What It Is

As in polygyny, this is a marriage-based relationship. There are different types of polyandry that are practiced in various cultures around the world. Here are some of the most common types of polyandry:

1. Fraternal Polyandry: In this type of polyandry, a woman marries multiple brothers at the same time. This is commonly practiced in Tibet, where the practice helps to keep the family property intact and prevent it from being divided among multiple heirs.

2. Non-Fraternal Polyandry: In this type of polyandry, a woman marries multiple men who are not related to each other. This is less common than fraternal polyandry and is practiced in certain parts of India, where it is believed to help reduce the number of men in the population and to control resources.

3. Group Marriage Polyandry: In this type of polyandry, a group of men and women form a marriage unit, and all members of the group are married to each other. This type of marriage is rare and is usually found in small, isolated communities.

4. Serial Polyandry: In this type of polyandry, a woman marries multiple husbands one after the other. This is commonly practiced in certain parts of Africa, where it is believed to help women gain social and economic status.

It is worth noting that polyandry is not as common as polygyny (where a man is allowed to have multiple wives) and is often practiced in cultures where resources are scarce or where women are highly valued.

What It Isn't

This is not about a woman who has no control over her sexual desires, as some in the patriarchy would like to suggest. As noted above, it is traditional in some cultures, and the history of culture can become today's modern ways of doing things.

How It Functions

The ways in which polyandrous marriages function can vary depending on the specific cultural context and the preferences of the individuals involved.

In some cases, polyandrous marriages may be arranged, with brothers or other male relatives sharing a wife in order to maintain property or family lineages. In other cases, a woman may choose to have multiple husbands for various reasons, such as to increase the support she receives or to fulfill sexual desires. In some cultures, polyandry may be motivated by economic considerations, as it allows multiple brothers to share a single wife and pool their resources. In other cultures, it may be motivated by social or religious reasons.

One common way that polyandrous marriage's function is through a system of rotation, where the husbands take turns spending time with their wife and sharing household responsibilities. This can help to ensure that each husband has equal access to the wife and that no one feels left out or neglected.

Polyandrous marriages can also involve different levels of intimacy and emotional connection between the wife and her husbands. Some relationships may be primarily sexual, while others may involve deep emotional bonds and romantic love.

In other cases, polyandrous relationships can be hierarchical, with one husband occupying a higher status or having more authority than the others. Alternatively, all husbands may have equal status and rights within the relationship.

One important aspect of polyandry is the issue of paternity. Because a woman may have multiple sexual partners, it can be difficult to determine the biological father of any given child. In some polyandrous societies, this is resolved through social conventions or beliefs, such as assigning paternity to the eldest or most dominant husband or viewing all the husbands as the father of any children born to the wife. Of course, in countries where modern medicine is available, a simple paternity test will decide.

Overall, polyandry is a complex social and cultural phenomenon that can take many different forms and serve a variety of functions, depending on the context in which it is practiced.

Mindset

As women have become more in tune and aware of their own desires as women, they have chosen to express them in ways that are best for them.

The mindset of participating in a polyandrous love style will be a matter of traditional versus modern. As most people who are reading this book, I believe, are from the USA, they will likely lean towards a more modern take instead of a cultural norm as in the societies of Nepal and India.

A more modern take would be that a monogamous woman discovers that the other side of polygyny is polyandry and that she would like to have more than one husband for various reasons. Those can be... she has more love to give and wants more love than she is receiving. It may initially be a sexual attraction that turns into a more deeply rooted relationship. It could be the agreement between her and her initial husband that having another man and income contributing to what they are building makes sense for their future. She has found a man that offers love differently than her initial husband, and she would enjoy that kind of love and attention being a part of her life as well. As in polygyny, one of the marriages must exist legally for this to be polyandrous when the additional partner comes into the relationship.

Examples

Most recently, the founders of Progressive Love Academy, Kenya and Carl Stevens, along with her second partner/husband, Tiger, premiered on TLC's Seeking Brother Husbands. Kenya and Carl have been together for more than twenty-five years and polyamorous for more than seventeen years. They have both had commitment ceremonies with their additional partners, making them both polygynous and polyandrous. Kenya is also polyamorous, as she also has additional lovers outside of their committed unions.

Examples of polyandry benefits are very similar to polygyny benefits:

1. Financial resource sharing: By sharing a wife, husbands can pool their resources and jointly support the family. This can enhance the economic well-being of the household and offer more income and opportunities to build wealth.

2. Division of chores: Polyandrous relationships can lead to a better division of chores and labor among men and women. With

multiple husbands, the responsibility for providing resources, childcare, and household chores can be shared, allowing those who may have special skills to take on different tasks based on their skill levels and interests. This can lead to increased efficiency and productivity within the family.

3. Enhanced sexual satisfaction: Polyandry can offer women a variety of sexual experiences and partners, potentially leading to increased sexual satisfaction. With multiple husbands, women may have a wider range of sexual preferences fulfilled, which can contribute to overall relationship satisfaction and well-being. Because yes, women like variety in their sex lives as much as men.

4. Social cohesion and stability: Although this is less of a focus in the USA, in some societies, polyandry can contribute to social cohesion and stability. By creating kinship bonds among brothers or male relatives, polyandrous unions can strengthen social ties and foster cooperation within extended families. This can help maintain social order and reduce conflicts over resources and power.

CHAPTER 13

Defining "Polyamory"

Polyamory is a type of consensual non-monogamy in which individuals have multiple romantic and/or sexual relationships with the knowledge and consent of all parties involved.

What It Is

Polyamory is different from cheating or infidelity, as all parties are aware of and agree to multiple relationships. Polyamorous relationships can take many forms, such as triads (three people in a relationship), quads (four people), or networks (multiple people interconnected in various ways), also known as a polycule. Polyamorous relationships can take many forms, and there is no one "right" way to practice polyamory. However, there are some common elements that are important to understand when exploring polyamory.

What It Isn't

It is not an excuse for cheating or infidelity. It is not you deciding to 'be polyamorous' yet not letting your partner know that you are dating others. You tell others that you are dating and that you are polyamorous, but they don't know what that is or means, truly. But you may briefly explain that it means 'many loves' and that you enjoy dating and loving many people, and that it's all open. But you fail to mention the part about your primary partner not having a clue that you are 'poly'. This is still called cheating. Using the terms and movements of a polyamorous person without taking the responsibility of letting the people you are involved with know the situation is not poly. You date/fuck a partner who is married as one of your partners, but you don't take into consideration that they have not told their partners about you because they are cheating... that is not only not poly, it's unethical. You and all of your partners may know about this person as a partner of yours, but they have not told anyone about you... because they are cheating. There is a difference between privacy and secrecy, which we discuss later in the book.

How It Functions

Polyamory is a relationship style in which individuals have multiple romantic or sexual partners with the consent and knowledge of all parties involved.

One of the key elements of polyamory is open communication and authentic honesty between all parties involved. This means that partners must be willing to discuss their feelings, desires, and boundaries openly and honestly, and must be willing to listen to and respect the feelings, desires, and boundaries of their partners and sometimes their partners' partners.

Another important aspect of polyamory is the recognition that each relationship is unique and valuable in its own right. Polyamorous individuals recognize that it is possible to love and/or be 'in love' with multiple people at the same time, and that each relationship can bring something different and special into their lives.

Mindset

Polyamorous relationships can take many different forms depending on the needs and preferences of the people involved. Here are some common ways that polyamorous relationships can be structured. As with every other love style in this book, none of these structures are designed to put you in a box. You can, at any time, combine any of the love styles. This is to show you what the options are so that you and/or your partners can decide what is best for you and your relationship(s). You can be poly/monogamous or poly/swinger or, as I am, open, swinger, poly, kinky. I don't like labels, so I do them all!

a. **Triads or "throuples"**: In a triad or "throuple," three people are in a relationship with each other, and each person is romantically and/or sexually involved with the other two. Triads can be closed, meaning they do not have additional relationships with others outside of the triad, or open, where they may take on other lovers or indulge in swinging. Sometimes only one of the three wants to take on an additional lover/partner. It is up to all the parties involved and their agreements. There are times when a triad may live together under the same roof (nesting), but it is not required.

b. **Quads**: Typically, a quad consists of four individuals who are all romantically and/or sexually involved with each other, forming a close-knit group or network of relationships. Each person within the quad may have varying degrees of emotional and physical connections with the others involved. The quad structure can take different forms depending on the preferences and dynamics of the individuals involved. For example, all four individuals may have equal relationships with each other, meaning they are all romantically and sexually involved with each other. Alternatively, the relationships within the quad may be interconnected in different ways. Some quads may involve two primary partnerships, where each person is primarily involved with one other person in the group, but there may still be some level of connection and involvement between all four individuals.

c. **V-shaped relationships**: In a V-shaped relationship, one person (the "hinge") is romantically involved with two other people (the "arms"), but the two arms are not romantically involved with each other. This too can be open or closed, depending on the agreement of the partners involved. This structure may or may not live under the same roof. As with the Triad, it is not a requirement.

d. **Polycule relationships**: This can involve multiple people in a complex network of relationships. For example, person A might be romantically involved with person B, who is also involved with person C, who is also involved with person D, and so on. In my opinion, polycules form almost accidentally. But it doesn't feel that way because those involved have similar intentions on how they want to love and be loved. So, as they each meet and expand their love styles, they bring others who are in alignment into the polycule.

e. **Solo polyamory**: is a relationship orientation where a person maintains multiple romantic and/or sexual relationships but does not prioritize the establishment of a primary or nesting partnership. In solo polyamory, individuals value autonomy, independence, and personal growth, and often prioritize their own individual needs over the needs of any specific partner or relationship. This can mean that they don't live with or marry any of their partners, and they do not seek to create a hierarchy of relationships.

f.   **Polyfidelity**: In a polyfidelitous' relationship, a group of people agree to be sexually and/or romantically exclusive to each other. This can look like a closed triad or quad, or a larger group of people.

g.   **Kitchen table polyamory:** This style emphasizes a high degree of communication and friendship between all partners, to the extent that everyone feels comfortable sitting around the "kitchen table" together.

Honorable mention: Relationship Anarchy. Relationship anarchy is not 'poly' but falls under the umbrella of an ethical non-monogamous love style. I've heard it in relation to polyamory, but it is not. It is a philosophy that emphasizes the importance of individual autonomy and the rejection of social norms and expectations around relationships. Relationship anarchists believe that all relationships should be voluntary, consensual, and based on mutual respect and communication, rather than being defined by traditional labels and hierarchies. Relationship anarchists may have multiple romantic and/or sexual relationships, but they reject the idea that any one relationship should take priority over others.

These are just a few examples of the many ways that polyamorous relationships can be structured. The most important thing is that all partners communicate clearly and honestly with each other about their needs, boundaries, and desires, and work together to create a relationship structure that works for everyone involved.

Example

Alex Porter and his wife Shalaun and girlfriend Shantell are content creators and influencers surrounding polyamory. Alex has been married to Shalaun for 23 years and has been with Shantell for 6 years. He and Shalaun were married for 17 years before he opened up his marriage to polyamory. Their relationship is a successful one although they transitioned from monogamy to ethical non-monogamy through infidelity. It is one of the more challenging ways and sometimes least successful ways to enter ENM. When so much trust has been lost it will take an abundance of trust to rebuild the first relationship and expand into the new one. But with healing and authentic honesty with regards to how and why the infidelity occurred, it can happen as they have proven. IG:@portahfamily

CHAPTER 14

Communication: *Is Better in the Morning Learning to Use Your Words, Authentically*

I was at a business conference when I heard business and life coach Myron Golden state, "The challenge most people have with communication is thinking that it already happened." We all know it and we all say it: having good communication is important to the health of the relationship. But what is considered "good communication" can be somewhat subjective, although it should not be. Many don't realize that effective communication is a skill and if it is a skill, it can be learned. No one is born knowing how to communicate effectively.

When you transition into ethical non-monogamy, you begin to learn to be authentically honest with your partners. You begin to express your needs, wants, and desires as well as your disappointments, hurt, and assumptions as you shed what you believed to be effective communication within the monogamous world.

In monogamy, communication can be half-assed, at best, and barely there at its worst. In monogamy, we can mistakenly believe that it is best to keep our joys and desires to ourselves. Mainly because we don't want to hurt, disappoint, or upset our partners, sometimes at the risk of our own happiness or satisfaction. We can keep our unsettled resentment to ourselves so that we don't make our partners feel less than, insecure, or even hurt because our needs are not being met.

Let's look at the foundation of effective communication to get a clear understanding of the skills that will assist you in building a deeper relationship with your partner(s) and others.

Three Elements of Communication

Most of us have learned that it's not what you say, it's how you say it. But the fact of the matter is that the "how" is our body language, which is 55% responsible for how we communicate. Only 38% is the tone of voice, and 7% is the actual words. So, in today's world of technology, what does that mean when we are constantly texting and emailing? It means that a lot of our communication is being misconstrued. Sure, we can use bold letters or emojis, but nothing is more effective than face-to-face communication. If you are texting with your partner and seem to be misunderstanding each other, after three exchanges and it is still not clear... pick up the phone. If you cannot be in person, then FaceTime, Zoom, or WhatsApp video. And at the very least, when you talk on the phone, you have tone of voice and words. You can at least hear the tone and you can hear where the miscommunication is and how they feel about the words coming out of your mouth.

Another important thing to take into consideration is that you, as the speaker, are 100 percent responsible for the words that are coming out of your mouth. Many times, when we are "communicating," we say what we say and then we say, "OK," and then we walk away. That's not communicating... that's dumping all your words out and moving on.

Taking the time to ask your partner to repeat back what they thought they heard you say is one way to clarify and/or correct what they believe you said. You can put the responsibility on yourself by saying, "I'm working on being a better communicator. Could you tell me, in your own words, what you thought I just said? I just want to make sure that I'm clear." At that point, you sit and you listen to understand, not just hear. When they are done, you now have an opportunity to clarify or correct them based on what they thought they heard. Here is a better understanding of the differences between the two words.

Clarifying vs. Correcting

Clarifying and correcting are two different actions, although they are related to improving understanding and communication.

Clarifying means to make something clearer or easier to understand. It involves asking questions or providing more information to help someone understand what was previously unclear. Clarification can be used to remove ambiguity or confusion or to make sure that everyone is on the same page.

Correcting, on the other hand, means to fix something that was wrong or inaccurate. It involves pointing out errors or mistakes in something that has been said or written and then providing the correct information. Correction can be used to prevent misunderstanding and ensure accuracy.

In summary, clarifying helps to enhance understanding, while correcting helps to improve accuracy.

The Communications Loop

We all have filters and barriers that can hinder our communication. Filters are internal factors such as culture, age, gender, language, body type, education, sexual orientation, past experiences, politics, disability, or personality. Barriers are external factors such as temperature (of the room/space), lights, noise, chairs, plants. Both filters and barriers affect how well your communication is given and received. Within the communication loop, the sender sends their message, and the receiver receives it. As stated, the sender is 100 percent responsible for the words that are coming out of their mouth. But as the receiver, you are 100 percent responsible for the words that you are receiving. So if the sender doesn't ask for clarification, the receiver must ask for it. You do the same by saying to the speaker (sender), "I want to make sure that I understood what you just said to me. I'd like to repeat back to you what I thought you just said so I can make sure that I am clear." This goes back to the clarifying and correcting scenario. So much time could be saved if we would take a few moments and get clarification and/or make the correction.

Word Lag

On average, we speak 150 to 200 words per minute. But we listen (process) between 600 and 1,000 words per minute. So, what is the result... word lag? In between the time the words come out of someone's mouth, we have already processed them and are starting to form our response. If we are starting to form our response, we are not listening. One of the most difficult things to do is to listen to understand and not listen to respond.

Incongruence

Incongruence is when your words do not match your body language. An example would be a person standing in front of you, head down, arms folded, and speaking in a very slow and monotone voice, but saying to you, "You are the most amazing person I've ever met in my life. I am thrilled to have met you and so excited to be with you." That is incongruence! Their body language and words just don't match up. When you are speaking to your partner (or about to), you want to set your intention and make sure that your body language matches the words that are coming out of your mouth. Remember, body language is 55% of how we communicate, and if they don't match, what kind of message are you sending?

Now that we have covered how to communicate, let's talk about what you want to communicate.

CHAPTER 15

How to talk to your partner about opening or expanding your relationship love style?

Set Your Intentions. Use Your Words.

Opening a relationship can be a complex and sensitive topic, and it's important to approach it with care and honesty. It is important to set your intentions, meaning, what do you want the outcome of this conversation to be? Are you expecting it to have a conclusion and agreement with this first conversation? Is this just a pre-conversation to "test the waters" of how your partner may feel? How serious are you about wanting a different love style than the one you currently have? Reviewing all the love styles under the umbrella of ethical non-monogamy, which one do you believe will be good for you and/or your partner? Is this a journey that you wish to embark on alone, or do you want to do this together? Know that once you open this conversation, you will not be able to "un-ring the bell". If you decide not to move forward with opening your relationship, know that it will forever be changed. Not in a good or bad way, but certainly different.

Before having that conversation, note that ethical non-monogamy will not fix your relationship! If your relationship is not stable or has not been stable for some time, opening it will not make it better. In fact, it will most likely make it worse by putting a magnifying glass on every crack and lead to a separation of ways. Do you understand the amount of time, effort, communication, honesty, and patience required to maintain multiple relationships? Even if you are only engaged in an ongoing sexual relationship with someone, is this something you genuinely wish to pursue? Ethical non-monogamy will not prevent you or your partner from cheating if either of you is inclined to cheat. It will not prevent you from lying to your partner if you are a habitual liar. It will simply afford you more freedom to engage in such behaviors. I highly recommend focusing on your current relationship, working on repairing and healing it, as well as improving yourself, before considering additional relationships. If you struggle with open and authentic communication with one partner, adding more people will only make it more challenging, not easier. Moreover, it is entirely unfair to involve another person in a relationship that lacks a solid foundation. Your additional partners have emotions, egos, and relationship goals just like you do, so it is crucial to consider their needs.

Below are some questions to ask yourself and/or your partner when contemplating ethical non-monogamy. Asking direct questions that invite non-judgmental and genuinely honest responses can facilitate a smoother transition for everyone involved. Will some of the answers be enlightening, disturbing, or even shocking? Possibly. Will you know how to proceed once you or your partner provides the answers? Yes.

1. Is opening a relationship a potential solution to address existing relationship issues?

2. Are you considering ethical non-monogamy as a means to salvage a struggling relationship, such as in cases of infidelity or compulsive sexual behavior?

3. Are you interested in having multiple sexual partners?

4. Do you prefer engaging in sexual activities separately or with your partner?

5. Are you seeking casual sexual interactions or long-term emotional relationships through ethical non-monogamy?

6. Do you desire for your partners to be involved in your home life, or would you prefer to maintain some distance?

7. Are there any specific kinks or fantasies you would like to explore within ethical non-monogamy?

8. Is it possible to share intimate emotions with more than one person simultaneously?

9. Am I comfortable expressing my needs to my partner(s) within the context of ethical non-monogamy?

10. Am I okay with the idea of sharing my partner with others?

11. What boundaries should be established within the framework of ethical non-monogamy?

12. Am I capable of managing feelings of jealousy if they arise, and how will we address them?

To communicate your desire to open or expand your relationship to your partner, consider the following steps:

a. Reflect on your reasons first: It's essential to understand your motivations for wanting to open your relationship. Social media has become full of posts, stories, memes, and other people's relationships surrounding ethical non-monogamy. Has social media influenced your thoughts on this, as there are so many "pushing" the ENM lifestyle without substance? How have you been as a partner thus far? Have there been any instances of infidelity that could make your partner feel as though they would not be able to trust you with this type of "freedom"? Is it because you feel stifled or unfulfilled in your current arrangement? Or do you feel drawn to exploring relationships with other people? Be clear about what you hope to gain from opening your relationship so you can communicate it effectively. Do you know which love style is good for you? What if your partner is more interested in a different love style? For example, if you are open to swinging, but your partner is more interested in deeper relationships that include a more regular partner with dates and love included, how might you come to terms with those differences?

b. Choose the right time and place: Find a time and place where you and your partner can talk privately without distractions. Make sure you both have enough time to discuss the topic thoroughly without feeling rushed or interrupted. On the way to work before you rush out the door will not be a good time. Neither will right after a long day at work. Perhaps Saturday morning over breakfast or Sunday brunch. If you have kids, perhaps they could stay at a sitter the night before to give you a good amount of time to discuss. If you are tired or stressed from life, perhaps you should wait for a better day.

c. Be authentically honest and direct: I know you have heard this many times throughout the book, but it cannot be overemphasized. Being honest with yourself about what it is you desire is the best way to get what you desire. Living a life based on someone else's needs will not satisfy you. Authentic honesty refers to the practice of being truthful and genuine in one's communication with others while also being true to oneself. It involves expressing oneself in a way that is sincere, transparent, and based on one's true thoughts, feelings, and values. Authentic honesty goes beyond simply telling the truth. It also involves being willing to express one's vulnerabilities, limitations, and mistakes in a genuine and transparent manner. Be upfront and honest about your desire to open your relationship. Use "I" statements to express how you feel and avoid making accusations or assumptions (something we accept as facts without it being proven) about your partner's feelings. Remember to be respectful and understanding of their reaction, whether it's positive or negative. Your goal is to tell them what it is you have been thinking and considering.

d. Listen to your partner: Give your partner the opportunity to express their thoughts and feelings about your proposal. Be prepared to answer any questions they may have and give them time to process the information. Listen to understand, not to respond. If this is the first time this has ever come up, they may feel blindsided. It is not the time to tell them what is not right with their thinking. They may feel hurt, betrayed, or unwanted, or as stated in the chapter about being open, that they are 'not enough'. Don't push for a decision at this initial conversation. You are not, in a sense, asking for their permission to become ethically non-monogamous. But you may be asking them to join you on this journey. Or you may be embarking on this journey alone. Either way, you want to hold space for your partner while they process this new information. Allow them the space to ask all questions without a rebuttal to the question. This is the time to exercise patience. Everyone doesn't process information at the same rate and with the same understanding. Remember that this information is something that has been in your head and/or heart for some time. You had to initially process it yourself, for yourself. You had to come to terms with the fact that you want to change the direction and love style of your current relationship.

e. Discuss boundaries and expectations: If your partner is open to the idea, it's important to discuss boundaries and expectations for your new arrangement. Be clear about what is and isn't acceptable and agree on a plan for communicating about any concerns that may arise. Boundaries and expectations are going to vary based on the love style. An "Open don't ask, don't tell" arrangement will have distinctly different boundaries and expectations than a polyamorous relationship. Regardless of which style you choose, please note that when you first open your relationship, you may likely have many, many boundaries and expectations. Most people put up these boundaries because they believe they need to protect their relationship. As mentioned earlier, when my husband and I opened our relationship, our initial list of boundaries included:

1. No family, friends, co-workers, or hotel staff (we both traveled for work).

2. No one in the entire state of North Carolina.

3. No spending the night.

4. No getting emotionally involved.

5. Always use condoms.

By the time we were thirteen years into ENM, the only boundaries we had remaining were: no children and no animals. I kid, I kid! Everything on the list had been removed except the use of condoms. We came to realize that our relationship didn't need 'protecting'. We were Open and then eventually transitioned into a swinging lifestyle together. We have made long-lasting friendships and lovers, and nobody is going anywhere.

Here are some boundaries that I have heard others have in their love styles:

1. No kissing.

2. No cumming/finishing with the other person, even if I'm not there.

3. No cuddling after sex. When you are done, get up and put your clothes on.

4. No contact after the initial meeting, unless I am part of the call, text, or email.

   f. **Respect your partner's decision**: If your partner is not interested in opening the relationship, respect their decision.

You now must decide, for yourself, is this something that is a part of you? Meaning, is being ethically non-monogamous just a way to date others or is this a lifestyle choice for you? Only you know the answer, and there is no right or wrong way, only the way that feels deeply and authentically you. Opening your relationship is something that you would preferably do together. Remember that opening up a relationship is a decision that both partners must make together, and it's important to prioritize your partner's feelings and needs.

a. How to open yourself up to ethical non-monogamy as a single person.

Deciding to date or live the lifestyle as ethically non-monogamous as a single person has its own set of challenges. You would like to believe that because you don't have to discuss this decision with anyone and seek their agreement, that this would be such a simple transition. To some degree it is. But before you do, I encourage you to ask the same or questions of yourself that are listed above.

CHAPTER 16

Feeling all The Feels: Managing Emotions - The Good, The Bad, and The WTF?

You do not become exempt from your emotions just because you have decided to open or transition your relationship into ethical non-monogamy. You may experience lust, what feels like love, jealousy, anger, joy, insecurity, envy, and/or gratitude. Some of us experience them more deeply or more intensely than others. Learning how to manage your emotions is the goal, not eliminating them. It is okay to feel jealousy, envy, or fear of loss or rejection. It is okay to feel love and joy. It is what you do about those feelings and emotions that will determine how you navigate ethical non-monogamy. You are a human, having a human experience. Let's look at some of the emotions you may experience during your transition or within ENM.

Compersion

Compersion is a term often used in the context of ENM and especially within polyamorous relationships or open relationships to describe a positive emotional response that an individual experiences when their partner or loved one is involved in a romantic or sexual relationship with someone else. It is essentially the opposite of jealousy. It is to be happy for your partner's happiness. We practice compersion all the time with our friends and family. Your very best friend has been wanting and applying for a vice president (V.P.) position within their company for more than three years. They've applied two years in a row, and on this third try, they succeeded. They call you ecstatic with the news. You are overjoyed at the joy that they feel because you know how much it means to them to achieve this in their life. That... is compersion.

When someone feels compersion, they feel joy, happiness, and satisfaction in witnessing their partner's happiness and fulfillment with another person. They can genuinely appreciate and derive pleasure from their partner's experiences and connections with others. This emotional state is characterized by empathy, love, and a genuine desire for the well-being of all parties involved.

Compersion requires a high level of emotional maturity and open-mindedness, as it challenges societal norms and traditional ideas of monogamy. It not only involves open communication, trust, and the willingness to embrace multiple loving relationships simultaneously but also requires you to take your eyes and emotions off yourself and embrace the joy that your partner is experiencing.

It's important to note that compersion is not something that everyone experiences or desires. Different individuals have different emotional responses and relationship preferences. While compersion can be a positive and fulfilling experience for some people, it may not resonate with others, and that's perfectly okay too. Just as some people may not feel jealousy, some people may not feel compersion.

Fear of Loss

When our partners become involved, sexually, or romantically, a fear of loss can rise up within us. What if they like the other person more than they like me? What if the other person's sex is better than mine, so much so that my partner wants that sex more than mine? As I stated above, nobody can steal someone who doesn't want to go. And you cannot make someone stay that is ready to leave.

Jealousy

Being 'jealous' is one emotion that constantly comes up when discussing why one person would not be able to transition into ENM. Understand that just because you have an emotion doesn't mean that you have to act upon it right then and there. When you begin to feel jealous, treat it like the "check engine" indicator in your car. It's a signal that something is out of balance, and it deserves your attention. It is your responsibility to examine your own thoughts and emotions to identify the source of these feelings. Remember, people don't do things to you or against you; they do things for themselves. We tend to look at 'that person/thing' over there that is doing this thing to me to 'make me' jealous. They are not intentionally trying to make you jealous. In fact, their actions most likely have absolutely nothing to do... with you.

But there are many things that can trigger the emotion of jealousy, such as:

1. Your partner's partner (aka metamour)

2. Less time with your partner

3. Something tangible, i.e., that thing over there, that occurrence, this moment.

4. Assumptions (things we accept as fact without proof)

5. Possessiveness – You really want that thing, person, event, feeling, fill-in-the-blank for yourself.

6. Low self-esteem – You are afraid that you are not really good enough.

7. Control – You want your partner to do what you want them to do... in a way that YOU want them to do, when it works for YOU.

8. Rational fear

9. More solo child-care

10. Cowboys/Cowgirls

11. Vulnerability

Jealousy can be triggered in a variety of ways. It can be disruptive or constructive or a mix of both. Some people don't get jealous as they react with compersion (the opposite of jealousy). But you can learn to feel the jealousy. You can learn to express jealousy in a way that does not punish your partner or interfere with your partner's relationships with other people. You can learn to self-soothe and calm yourself down and to tolerate jealousy.

So, how do you deal with this intense emotion? Focus on the fact that the mind controls the body. Say to yourself: "I CAN STAND IT." You can use this statement to calm yourself down and soothe yourself. These four words will help counter the cultural conditioning that we are powerless to handle jealousy constructively. Society says jealousy is an irresistible force. It's in the movies and television. We see it in social media where a woman is slapping a man for simply admiring a beautiful woman. Jealousy is not a requirement within a relationship to prove love. Just because you are in a committed relationship doesn't mean your ability or desire for a beautiful man or woman goes away. And the fact that the monogamous culture states that you should never have any desires or Christianity says that desire is evil is pure... bullshit. You are a human, with emotions, desires, lust, and love. Committing to one or many people will not make those go away, and to ask your partner to push those emotions away due to your insecurities and/or jealousy is... well, wrong and immature. If you have children or have ever seen a toddler have a temper tantrum, as they get older, they learn to soothe themselves and control their emotions and use their words instead of the tantrum. No one is saying that you will not have emotions. I am saying that you can learn to control your emotions. Some of you have chosen not to control them. 9

Just as you can learn to control your emotions, believe that your partner(s) have that same ability to control themselves and will not run off with anyone who admires them or whom they find desirable. Nobody can steal someone who doesn't want to go. And you can't make someone stay if they are ready to leave. We have all seen men with mistresses who have one to two children and have been in the relationship for ten years, threatening to leave him if he doesn't leave his wife. He says, "I'm not leaving my wife no matter what." On the opposite side of that, we have seen women who have left their husbands when they were eight months pregnant. There isn't anything you can do about either situation. So, putting yourself in a full-on emotional downward spiral does nothing for you or your relationship.

Breathe deeply, exhale completely, and repeat: "I can stand it." The mind controls the body.

I understand that it can be challenging to stay calm when these skills are still new. Old habits can creep in and hijack your brain. Here are some strategies for dealing with jealousy when you feel it rising up in you:

1. Remain silent and avoid taking any action. Just because you have an emotion doesn't mean you have to act upon it right then and there.

2. Practice the ability to endure discomfort. Learn to sit with that uncomfortable feeling.

3. Remind yourself that you have the strength to withstand this feeling.

4. Create distance between yourself and the situation.

5. Step away momentarily and say, "I need to hydrate or refill my drink."

6. Or, "I need to excuse myself to use the restroom; I'll return shortly."

7. Or, "I need both water and a restroom break."

8. Or, state: "This is a challenging situation. I need time to process, calm down, and gain perspective. I value this relationship. I'll be

back soon," assuring the other person that you're not turning away from them.

You have bought yourself some time! Perhaps write your feelings down on a digital notepad on your phone. Are you feeling rejected, disrespected, or unloved? Is the other person cuter, sexier, younger, or do you feel like your partner no longer needs/wants you?

Observe what is really happening. Turn away from the feelings and just focus on the facts. What has actually transpired? Who were the players? What are your current pre-existing agreements? Did all the players know?

What are you thinking? When I refer to all of the players knowing, sometimes people outside of your relationship have absolutely no idea what your agreements or boundaries are with you and your partner because no one took the time to use their words.

I once coached a couple who had a fallout because they had played with (had sex as swingers) a single woman, and afterwards the single woman contacted the husband directly. The wife was so mad she put the husband on a timeout within the lifestyle for about six months. When I asked what upset her about the woman contacting him, especially since she knew her and had already played with her. She stated, "Because she should have come through me." I asked, "How was the single woman supposed to know that she was supposed to go through you? Did you tell her that that was you and your husband's agreement?" She said, "No." And since she didn't know, why did you punish your husband because the woman called him? Why did you not call the woman and just let her know the first time she called? That would have saved you time, and you would not have been upset. Yes, her husband could/should have told her. That is a separate conversation. I'm trying to make the point that the woman didn't do anything against her, and even her husband didn't do anything against her. This is also not the first woman that they have played with who is allowed to call him directly. So, he was a bit shocked that she was so upset about this particular woman. When setting boundaries, leave room for the possibility that someone may come along and trigger you in a way that overrides your logic. Knowing that this trigger could happen can help you keep your own emotions under control.

We decide whether to talk about our jealousy... or not. We may decide there is nothing to talk about. It came and went, and we're over it. Challenge the assumption that the feeling of jealousy should be avoided at all costs. Trying to avoid a natural human feeling such as jealousy is like telling ourselves that we are wrong to be normal. Words matter, and it's good to know when to bring up a subject. You are responsible for you, your health, and your happiness. If you want a hug, don't start an argument. Do you want to be 'right' or connect with your partner? Do you want to win or increase the love and happiness that you have in your life and with your partner(s)?

Use Your Words. Communicating how you're feeling is the best and only way to get past what you are feeling. As stated earlier, it doesn't have to happen at the exact moment that you feel it. Some conversations are just... better in the morning.

Know when to hold 'em – Push the pause button on conflict. Regulate emotions – Calm down before communicating and make it easier for your partners to regulate their emotions. B.N.C. Perhaps you need a Blowjob, a Nap, or a Cookie? Remember your relationship goals. Slow down and think before you speak. Giving voice to conflict. Conflict is not negative or positive, it just... is.

Jealousy vs Envy

Jealousy and envy are two distinct emotions that are often used interchangeably, but they have different meanings and implications. There are times when a person is envious and not jealous, but here's an explanation of jealousy versus envy:

Jealousy: Jealousy typically arises in situations involving a perceived threat to a valued relationship or possession. It occurs when someone fears losing something they already possess, such as a romantic partner, a close friend, or a material possession. Jealousy is often accompanied by feelings of insecurity, possessiveness, and the desire to protect what one already has. For example, a person might feel jealous when they see their partner spending time with someone else or when a colleague receives recognition for their work instead of them. Jealousy is rooted in a sense of fear or anxiety about potential loss.

Envy, on the other hand, arises when someone desires what another person has and wishes to possess it for themselves. It involves a feeling of discontent or resentment towards another person's qualities, achievements, possessions, or circumstances. Envy can stem from a sense of inferiority or the belief that one's own life is lacking in comparison to others. For instance, a person might feel envious when they see a friend's new car, a coworker's promotion, or a neighbor's luxurious house. Envy is often characterized by a desire to attain or surpass what another person has.

New Relationship Energy

New Relationship Energy (NRE) is a term used to describe the intense emotional and psychological excitement that often accompanies the beginning stages of a new romantic or sexual relationship. It refers to the feelings of infatuation, passion, and novelty experienced when forming a connection with a new partner. It is the butterflies that you get when you become connected with someone new! It almost feels like love, and you just buzz with joy every time they call or text you! It can be a positive and exhilarating experience, like the honeymoon phase of a monogamous relationship.

Some characteristics of NRE include:

1. **Intense emotions:** During NRE, people often experience heightened emotions, such as euphoria, obsession, and an overwhelming desire to spend time with their new partner.

2. **Increased focus and energy:** People under the influence of NRE tend to invest significant time and energy into the new relationship, which can sometimes lead to a temporary decrease in attention or availability for other partners or responsibilities.

3. **Idealization and projection:** The new partner may be seen through rose-colored glasses, with their flaws overlooked or minimized. There is a tendency to project positive qualities onto the new partner, creating an idealized image.

4. **Sexual excitement:** NRE often brings about a surge in sexual desire and exploration, leading to a heightened sense of intimacy and passion, willing to try new things (anal? sure), new toys, new positions (sex outside on the balcony? sure).

While NRE can be a thrilling and transformative experience, it is essential to navigate it consciously and ethically within the framework of non-monogamy. It is very easy to get caught up in the excitement of it all and begin to neglect your current partners by reducing the amount of time with them and/or attention to them. It is crucial to maintain open communication with all partners involved and ensure that existing relationships are nurtured and supported despite the excitement of new connections.

One of the most important things to realize is that this feeling wears off. It could take two weeks, two months, or two years, depending on the amount of time spent with the new partner. Understand that desire comes from the unknown and that love comes from the known. Because you don't know this person, your desire is strong to get to know them. So, this overwhelming feeling to be constantly in touch with them is not... love... it is desire. It takes time to be 'in love'. So, this is not the time to make life-altering decisions with your rose-colored glasses on. Just take a logical deep breath and stay the course of getting to know them. I have to admit NRE is a great burst of oxytocin, and some ENM people have openly confessed that they love NRE and purposely hop from one new relationship to another for a never-ending shot of it.

Tolerance and unconditional love are two distinct concepts, although they are related to each other.

Tolerance refers to the ability to accept and endure something that one dislikes or disagrees with, without necessarily agreeing with it. It can involve recognizing and respecting the rights and opinions of others, even if they differ from one's own. Tolerance often involves a degree of patience, understanding, and empathy towards others.

Unconditional love, on the other hand, refers to a type of love that is not dependent on any conditions or expectations. It involves loving someone for who they are, without judgment or the need for them to change. Unconditional love involves acceptance, forgiveness, and a deep sense of compassion towards others.

Some of us are tolerating the behavior of our partners and believing that it is unconditional love. You and your partner(s) are not attached at the hip. Meaning that if there is something that you want more or less in your relationship, use your words. You and only you are responsible for your happiness.

Although tolerance and unconditional love share some similarities, there are some important differences between them. Tolerance may involve putting up with something that one does not agree with, whereas unconditional love involves accepting and loving someone regardless of their flaws or mistakes. Additionally, tolerance can be a more passive approach, while unconditional love is an active choice to love someone for who they are. When deciding to enter into ENM, doing it for the right reasons, which are your right reasons, is what matters most.

CHAPTER 17

Consent

C onsent is an important aspect of ethical non-monogamy, just as it is in any type of relationship. It is important that we don't assume consent based on past relationships or past consensual agreements. When we transition into ENM, we sometimes believe that what was okay with us in our monogamous relationship will automatically transition over, and it is not always the case. Try to remember that these are new relationships, even the one you are in with your partner becomes 'new' because you have never been ethically non-monogamous before with this partner. Here are some ways to practice consent in ethical non-monogamy:

1. **Open and Honest Communication**: Establish open lines of communication with all involved parties. Discuss boundaries, expectations, desires, and concerns openly and honestly. Make sure everyone has the opportunity to express their needs and feelings.

2. **Prioritize Ongoing Consent**: Consent is not a one-time event but an ongoing process. Check in regularly with your partners to ensure that boundaries and desires are still being respected. Consent can change over time, so it's essential to have ongoing conversations.

3. **Negotiate Boundaries**: Clearly define boundaries and agreements with all parties involved. Discuss what is acceptable and what is not, both in terms of physical intimacy and emotional connections. Be willing to listen and adjust boundaries as needed.

4. **Give and Receive Affirmative Consent**: Obtain explicit and enthusiastic consent before engaging in any sexual or intimate activities with your partners. Likewise, ensure that your partners feel comfortable and supported in expressing their desires or limits.

5. **Respect Personal Autonomy**: Recognize that each individual has the right to make their own decisions about their bodies and relationships. Respect their autonomy and never pressure or coerce someone into any activities they are uncomfortable with.

6. **Be Mindful of Power Dynamics**: Consider the power dynamics at play in your relationships and be mindful of any imbalances. Be aware of how your actions or decisions may impact others and strive for fairness and equality.

7. **Regularly Reflect and Check-In**: Set aside time to reflect on your relationships, practices, and agreements. Revisit and adjust boundaries as needed. Regular check-ins can help maintain consent and ensure the well-being of everyone involved.

8. **Educate Yourself**: Continuously educate yourself about ethical non-monogamy, consent, and healthy relationship practices. Stay informed about the latest research, resources, and community discussions to enhance your understanding and skills. Buy additional books, look up YouTube videos, and/or book a coaching session. There is no reason not to continue to find ways to have the relationship that you desire.

Remember, ethical non-monogamy is unique to each individual and relationship. It is not a one-size-fits-all type of love style, hence the differences listed earlier in the book. It is crucial to communicate openly, respect boundaries, and prioritize consent to create a healthy and consensual environment for all parties involved.

Cowgirls/Cowboys

You may or may not have heard this term in the polyamory or the swinger community. They are what some consider the reason ENM has a bad name. In the context of the polyamory community, the terms "cowboy" and "cowgirl" are used to describe certain behaviors or tendencies exhibited by individuals who practice non-monogamous relationships. However, it's important to note that not everyone uses these terms, and they are not universally accepted or used by everyone within the polyamory community.

Cowboy: A "cowboy" typically refers to someone who engages in unethical or exploitative behavior within the realm of polyamory. This term is often used to describe individuals who pursue multiple romantic or sexual relationships with a disregard for the feelings, boundaries, or consent of their partners. Cowboys may manipulate or pressure others into participating in relationships, prioritize their own desires over the well-being of their partners, or engage in deceptive practices.

Cowgirl: Similarly, a "cowgirl" is someone who exhibits behavior similar to a cowboy, but the term specifically refers to women who engage in such behavior. It is worth noting that the use of gendered terms like "cowgirl" is not universally embraced, as it reinforces gender stereotypes and can be exclusionary.

Also note that the terms "cowboy" and "cowgirl" are often used to criticize or highlight problematic behavior within the polyamory community. Many individuals in the polyamory community prioritize ethical non-monogamy, which emphasizes open communication, consent, and respect for all parties involved. The vast majority of polyamorous individuals do not engage in exploitative or unethical behavior and strive to build healthy and consensual relationships. But these types of people do exist, just as you will find cheaters and other unethical people 'hiding in plain sight,' under the umbrella of ENM. They will get enough knowledge about the community to use the terminology to lure in someone who doesn't know and exploit that person, telling them that this is how ENM functions. They hunt the ill-informed and take advantage of the lack of knowledge about ENM.

CHAPTER 18

Setting Boundaries

Setting boundaries in ethical non-monogamy is crucial for maintaining healthy and respectful relationships. Here are some steps you can follow to establish and communicate boundaries within ethical non-monogamy:

1. **Setting Expectations:** Set the expectations that your boundaries will be met. Go into the conversation with the intention to make the relationship work. Setting the expectation gives you clarity with regards to understanding:

   a. Conflict happens when expectations differ.

   b. Expect to be respected.

   c. Refusing to take blame.

   d. Finding and maintaining your own identity.

   e. Avoiding co-dependency

   f. Asking for space.

2. **Self-reflection**: Take the time to understand your own needs, desires, and limitations. Reflect on what you're comfortable with and what may trigger feelings of insecurity or jealousy. This self-awareness will help you communicate your boundaries effectively.

3. **Open and honest communication**: Initiate an open and honest conversation with your partner(s) about your boundaries. Clearly express your feelings, concerns, and expectations regarding non-monogamy. Encourage them to share their thoughts and boundaries as well.

4. **Active listening**: Pay attention to your partner(s) when they express their boundaries. Listen attentively, validate their feelings, and try to understand their perspective without judgment or defensiveness. Make sure you're creating a safe and non-judgmental space for open communication.

5. **Negotiation and Compromise**: Non-monogamous relationships require negotiation and compromise. Discuss where your boundaries overlap or conflict and work together to find mutually satisfying solutions. Remember that boundaries can evolve and change over time, so ongoing communication is vital.

6. **Saying No Is An Emotional Boundary**: No is a complete sentence. If you are unable to say no, there are other ways to say no, without saying no. You can say:

   a. That doesn't work for me.

   b. Let me get back to you. (and don't get gack to them)

   c. I'm not available.

   d. I can't answer that right now.

7. **Be Specific**: When discussing boundaries, be as specific as possible. Vague statements like "I want to feel respected" may have different interpretations. Instead, provide concrete examples of behaviors or situations that may cross your boundaries. Clear, specific boundaries leave less room for misunderstandings.

8. **Considerations for Different Relationships**: If you're involved in multiple relationships, be mindful that each relationship may have its own unique boundaries. Discuss and negotiate

boundaries with each partner individually to address their specific needs and concerns.

9. **Regular Check-ins**: Regularly revisit and reassess your boundaries. Set aside time to check in with your partner(s) and openly discuss whether any adjustments are needed. As your relationships and dynamics change, so might your boundaries.

10. **Respect and Consent**: Respect the boundaries set by your partner(s) and ensure you obtain explicit consent before engaging in any activities that could potentially breach those boundaries. Consensual and respectful behavior is vital to ethical non-monogamy.

11. **Personal Responsibility**: Take personal responsibility for upholding your own boundaries and respecting those of your partner(s). Actively communicate your needs and concerns while being mindful of the needs and concerns of others. Strive to maintain a healthy balance between personal autonomy and consideration for others.

12. **Seek Support if Needed**: If you're finding it challenging to navigate boundaries in ethical non-monogamy, consider seeking support from a therapist, counselor, or coach experienced in non-monogamous relationships. They can provide guidance and help you navigate any difficulties that arise.

The Importance of Personal Boundaries

Personal boundaries play a crucial role in maintaining a healthy and fulfilling life which include the various aspects of personal boundaries, including the right to privacy, the right to change your mind, and the right to your own time.

One fundamental aspect of personal boundaries is the right to privacy. Everyone has the right to safeguard their personal information, thoughts, and emotions. Respecting others' boundaries by refraining from prying or invading their privacy is essential for maintaining healthy relationships and fostering trust. We have been led to believe that our partners must share their every thought with us, which is not true.

Another significant element of personal boundaries is the right to change your mind. It is natural for individuals to reassess their beliefs, opinions, and decisions over time. Embracing the freedom to change one's mind without fear of judgment or repercussion allows for personal growth and self-discovery.

Additionally, the right to your own time is paramount. Each person should have the autonomy to manage their time and allocate it according to their needs and priorities. Setting aside time for self-care, hobbies, and personal pursuits is essential for overall well-being and maintaining a healthy work-life balance.

Furthermore, it is crucial to address the need to handle negative energy. Establishing and maintaining personal boundaries can help protect oneself from toxic or draining situations. Recognizing when boundaries have been crossed and taking appropriate action to safeguard one's emotional and mental well-being is of utmost importance.

Moreover, personal boundaries extend to various aspects of life, including the freedom to express sexual, physical, and spiritual boundaries. Individuals have the right to establish and communicate their comfort levels and boundaries in these areas. Respecting and honoring these boundaries is vital for fostering healthy relationships and promoting mutual consent and respect.

Finally, personal boundaries also encompass the rights to material possessions. Everyone has the right to own and protect their belongings. Respecting others' property rights and seeking consent before using or accessing their possessions is an important aspect of personal boundaries and demonstrating consideration and respect.

The Downside of Not Setting Boundaries

It drags down your self-esteem. You develop unsettled resentment towards others, allowing them to tell you what is best for you and how you should feel about it. Your inability to say "no" makes people less responsible. You start to feel run over all the time. We don't know how to handle someone who is hurt by our boundaries. We feel selfish when we use our boundaries.

In conclusion, personal boundaries are essential for maintaining a balanced and fulfilling life. By acknowledging and respecting the rights and freedoms associated with personal boundaries, individuals can cultivate healthier relationships, enhance their well-being, and lead a more authentic and fulfilling life.

Privacy vs. Secrecy

Privacy and secrecy play different roles in the context of ethical non-monogamy. While privacy can be important for maintaining personal boundaries and protecting the privacy of individuals involved, secrecy generally undermines the ethical principles of open communication, honesty, and informed consent that are fundamental to ethical non-monogamy.

Privacy in Ethical Non-Monogamy: Privacy refers to the right to keep certain aspects of one's personal life or relationships confidential. In the context of ethical non-monogamy, privacy can be valued and respected to maintain personal boundaries. Individuals may choose to keep specific details about their relationships, sexual activities, or personal preferences private and not disclose them to others, including their partners or people within their social circle. Respecting privacy in these instances involves understanding and honoring the individual's wishes regarding what they choose to share or keep private.

In ethical non-monogamy, privacy can serve various purposes, such as protecting individuals from discrimination, maintaining professional reputations, or preserving personal autonomy. For example, someone might choose not to disclose their non-monogamous relationship status at work to avoid potential discrimination or prejudice.

Secrecy in Ethical Non-Monogamy: Secrecy, on the other hand, involves actively withholding information or intentionally keeping certain aspects of one's relationships hidden from others involved. Secrecy contradicts the principles of open communication, honesty, and informed consent that are central to ethical non-monogamy. Secretive behavior can lead to feelings of betrayal, mistrust, and harm to relationships.

In ethical non-monogamy, secrecy can occur when one partner engages in relationships or sexual activities without the knowledge or consent of their other partners. This can include engaging in secret affairs or hiding relationships from existing partners. Such secrecy can undermine the foundations of ethical non-monogamy, as it deprives all parties involved of the ability to make informed decisions about their relationships and consent to the dynamics at play.

I had such an event happen with a former partner. He had decided that he wanted to fluid bond (not use barriers) with a woman he had only been dating for a short time. He had informed me of their decision, and both were tested for STIs and shared their results with me, as he and I were fluid bonded. Some months later, he confessed that she was pregnant but did not want to tell me because it was their privacy. I said that that was not an example of privacy but secrecy because he did not share that information with me. Something like a baby will change the dynamics of our relationship in terms of available time and scheduling together. This was something to be discussed with me, not for me to make any decisions on their relationship, but to be able to emotionally express my feelings and determine whether I wanted to continue to be in a relationship with this new dynamic. I had the right to decide for myself whether to stay or go, and someone withholding information—secrets—should not make that decision for me. A decision was not made, as a few weeks after our discussion, she suffered a miscarriage.

Balancing Privacy and Transparency: Finding the right balance between privacy and transparency is crucial in ethical non-monogamy. Respecting an individual's privacy rights is important, but it should not be used as an excuse for secrecy or deception. Open and honest communication is vital in maintaining trust, fostering emotional intimacy, and ensuring that all parties involved have the necessary information to make informed decisions about their relationships.

Establishing clear agreements, boundaries, and guidelines regarding privacy and disclosure can help you navigate these challenges. Each individual and relationship may have different preferences and comfort levels regarding what they consider private and what they are willing to share. It is essential for all involved to engage in ongoing conversations, negotiate boundaries, and ensure that everyone's needs, desires, and boundaries are respected.

CHAPTER 19

Emotional and Physical Abuse in Ethical Non-Monogamy

Emotional and physical abuse can occur in any type of relationship, including ethical non-monogamous relationships. However, like any relationship structure, it does not guarantee that abuse will not occur.

It's important to remember that ethical non-monogamy is not inherently abusive. It's the *behavior of the individuals involved* that determines whether abuse is present. Here are some ways in which emotional and physical abuse may manifest in ethical non-monogamous relationships:

1. **Coercion and manipulation:** One partner may use manipulation or coercion to force or pressure their partners into agreeing to or participating in activities they are not comfortable with, such as having sex with others or engaging in specific relationships.

2. **Control and isolation:** An abusive partner may try to isolate their partners from other relationships or support networks, using tactics such as controlling their communication or limiting their freedom to pursue other connections. This can lead to emotional dependence and a lack of autonomy.

3. **Gaslighting:** Gaslighting is a form of psychological manipulation in which one person undermines the other's perception of reality, making them doubt their own feelings, memories, or judgments. This can be used by an abusive partner to control and diminish their partner's self-esteem and agency.

4. **Emotional manipulation:** Emotional abuse can involve insults, humiliation, belittlement, or constant criticism towards a partner's appearance, choices, or feelings. This behavior aims to demean and control the individual, damaging their self-worth and emotional well-being.

5. **Physical abuse:** Physical abuse can occur in any relationship, including ethical non-monogamous ones. It involves the use of physical force or violence, resulting in harm or injury to a partner. This behavior is never acceptable and should be taken seriously.

I had such a partner who, unbeknownst to me, was both emotionally and physically abusive to his primary partner and had been for several years before we met. Although they had opened their relationship prior to us meeting and dating, they were not polyamorous. As he took to the polyamorous lifestyle, reading many books and learning from me, he was telling his primary partner to just "get out board" because that was the way it was going to be. She eventually left him for almost a year, and it was during COVID that he and I bonded more intently. I had also left my own husband of twenty-five years, not due to our ethically non-monogamous relationship, but due to the fact that we were no longer kicking the can down the same road. Our kids were grown up and out of college and on their own. We had sold our home in North Carolina and moved to Miami, hoping for a fresh start. But it was not to be. I was also in two additional polyamorous relationships of four and two years.

As COVID kept us primarily in lockdown, there was a lot to learn. I had clear boundaries within our relationship, and he abided by them: don't cheat on me, don't lie to me, and don't put your hands on me. After ten months, his wife returned, and we all adjusted to a new dynamic as a V relationship. She and I became friends, and they began seeking therapy for their relationship. I had no idea about the level of abuse she had undergone with him, as I was not experiencing any. I knew he had issues with anger, but they were always directed away from me, and he was seeking therapy. Within that second year, he and I took a trip together, and that is where I discovered that he had been cheating and lying for the past few months. He had also met a new woman that he wanted to bring on as a submissive, and she was one of the main people he had been cheating with. Mind you, neither his wife nor I ever cared whom else he had sex with, but the boundary was always to use protection and be honest. A day after he was confronted with the lies, he turned on me and tried to choke me...to death. I fought my way out of the hotel room, ran to my friends, and he was put off of the resort. That was the beginning of the end of our relationship. He went to therapy, and I wanted very much to forgive him, but you can't un-ring a bell, the man almost killed me! The damage was done. He left the country, as did his wife, going to different countries. She and I kept in contact, and that is where I discovered that he had been abusive to her, this time using polyamory as a shield for all his emotional and physical abuse to her, using the very ways named above. We both left him and went to our own respective therapies so that we could move on and move on we did!

If you suspect that you or someone you know is experiencing abuse in an ethical non-monogamous relationship, it is crucial to seek help and support. Reach out to a trusted friend, family member, or a professional counselor who can provide guidance and assistance. Additionally, resources such as hotlines and organizations specializing in domestic violence can offer support and information tailored to your situation. Remember, everyone deserves to be in a safe and healthy relationship, regardless of the relationship structure they choose.

So, although ethical non-monogamy may be better than monogamy to many people, it is not without its own set of challenges. Becoming ethically non-monogamous will not make you less emotional, more in control of yourself, or even more truthful. It will, however, challenge you to be authentically honest with the one person it matters most to, and that person is you. At the end of the day, you and only you are responsible for your own happiness…and your own bullshit, because we all bring bullshit to the table!

Where I'm at now

Currently, I'm still open/swinging/poly/kinky. I've never been one for labels, so I claim them all! I'm living and working from Cancun, Mexico, and dating. I'm seeking cuddle buddies, travel buddies, nude beach buddies, and committed ethically non-monogamous relationships. I'm seeking a King (or three) who is authentically honest, emotionally, and financially stable, physically healthy, open-minded, sensual, a lover of travel, and ethically non-monogamous.

GLOSSARY

This glossary is contributed by Kato Cooks of <u>www.BlackandPoly.org</u>

ABUNDANT LOVE: The belief or philosophy that it is possible to love more than one person at the same time.

ADELPHOGAMY; also, FRATERNAL POLYANDRY, LEVIRATIC POLYANDRY: (Literally, adelphos brother + gamos marriage) A specific form of polyandry, practiced historically and occasionally still practiced in some portions of Tibet and Nepal, in which a set of brothers is married to the same woman.

ADULT BUFFET: Colloquial A specific type of group sex in which a group of consenting adults gets together for the purpose of sex, and each person in the group is free to have sex with any of the other members of the group he or she chooses. Usage: Originated with the swinging community; uncommon outside it.

AFAB: acronym for Assigned Female At Birth. See also AMAB.

AGAMY: (Literally, a no + gamos marriage) 1. A state or condition of not engaging in marriage, or more generally not engaging in marriage or reproduction. 2. Sociology Of or relating to a society with no recognized rules or prescriptions on marriage, or which does not recognize marriage at all.

AGENCY: "...the power people have to think for themselves and act in ways that shape their experiences and life trajectories. Agency can take individual and collective forms." https://www.thoughtco.com/agency-definition-3026036 With thanks to Jessica Burde of www.PolyamoryonPurpose.com

ALEXITHYMIA: (noun) is characterized by an inability to identify and express or describe one's feelings. Note: People with alexithymia typically display a lack of imaginative thought, have difficulty distinguishing between emotions and bodily sensations, and engage in logical externally oriented thought. The core characteristics of alexithymia are marked dysfunction in emotional awareness, social attachment, and interpersonal relating. Sometimes identified as a lack of feelings. (Thanks to Crystal Byrd Farmer.)

ALLOSEXUAL: Sexual attraction or behavior toward other people (as opposed to asexual). References: https://pianycist.wordpress.com/2012/08/08/allosexuel-and-allosexual/ and https://www.ncbi.nlm.nih.gov/pubmed/11912001. Defined in some places as extreme sexual appetite.

ALT.POLYCON (APC): A long-running annual convention of polyamorous people and people interested in polyamory, organized by the members of the UseNet newsgroup alt. polyamory and featuring a series of workshops, lectures, and so forth.

AMAB: acronym for Assigned Male At Birth. See also AFAB.

AMATORCULIST: "A little insignificant lover; a pretender to affection" (Samuel Johnson, A Dictionary of the English Language, 1755)

When one sees how pleased many people are to discover this word, one that finally will serve to provide an accurate description of some past lover, it is clear that amatorculist has not received the attention it deserves. The word is almost entirely unknown outside of dictionaries, and lexicographers seem to take a certain vicious glee in defining it. Joseph Wright, in his 1867 Dictionary of Obsolete and Provincial English defined the word as "A wretched lover or galant," and Nathan Bailey, in his 1736 dictionary, referred to it as "a trifling Sweet-heart, a general Lover." - Merriam-Webster.com

Example: Why, to tell you the truth, Squire Randal, as to the amatorculist, and his vertiginous gilt-piece of mutability, to such I have nothing to say, and with such I have nothing to do.

— James Hogg, Tales and Sketches, 1866

AMBIAMOROUS: Ambiamorous is an adjective used to describe someone who can enjoy being part of monogamous or polyamorous relationships. It is a combination of the Latin prefix ambi, meaning both, and amorous, from the Latin amor meaning love.

The term should not be confused with biamorous. While it may seem like a synonym, much like bisexual bridges the gap between heterosexual and homosexual, biamorous means "able to love more than one person." - from https://www.kinkly.com/definition/17238/ambiamorous See also: https://poly.land/2018/07/10/the-reasons-why-5-ambiamorous-people-chose-functional-monogamy/ (for a discussion) and http://amslang.enacademic.com/214/ambiamorous (where the word means 'loving both' with a different perspective). See also SWITCH, def. 2.

AMBIGUSWEETIE: Colloquial A partner with whom one's relationship is ambiguous or not clearly defined, often intentionally; as, We are not primary partners or secondary partners or simply friends, but rather ambigusweeties. Etymology: This term was coined by Chris Dunphy, from "ambiguous sweetie."

AMBW: AMBW is the Abbreviation of "Asian Men Black Women." Interacial relations and intimacy of Asian men with Black women. Be it dating, engaged, or married, so long they are coupled with male Asian descendent and Female African descendent, they fall under the category of AMBW. From https://www.urbandictionary.com/define.php?term=AMBW

AMOURETTE: The proper word to describe an insignificant love affair, rather than an insignificant lover. plural -s 1: a trifling or ephemeral love affair 2: a woman involved in a trifling love affair. Origin and Etymology of amourette French, from Old French, from amour + -ette

ANHEDONIA: noun A psychological condition characterized by inability to experience pleasure in normally pleasurable acts (Merriam-Webster Dictionary: https://www.merriam-webster.com/dictionary/anhedonia)

APC (initialism): See alt.polycon.

ASEXUAL: An asexual person (also "ace") is someone who does not experience sexual attraction. Aces can be any sex or gender or age or ethnic background or body type, can be rich or poor, can wear any clothing style, and can be any religion or political affiliation. www.whatisasexuality.com/intro/

AUTOPHOBIA: Fear of abandonment; also called monophobia, isolophobia, or eremophobia, is the specific phobia of isolation; a morbid fear of being abandoned, or a dread of being alone or isolated. Sufferers need not be physically alone, but just to believe that they are being ignored or unloved.

BDSM: BDSM is a variety of erotic practices that, in short, involve power exchange, role-playing, bondage, and other interpersonal dynamics. Given the wide range of practices, some of which may be engaged in by people who do not consider themselves as practicing BDSM, inclusion in the BDSM community or sub-cultures is usually dependent on self-identification and shared experience. Interest in BDSM can range from one-time experimentation to a lifestyle, and is sometimes referred to as a sexual identity/orientation. From www.bdsmwiki.info. The initialism stands for Bondage Dominant/Domination Slave/Submission/Sadism Masochism, depending on whom you ask. Our preferred resources include the renowned Orpheus Black (http://askOrpheusBlack.blogspot.com).

BIGAMY: (Literally, bi two + gamos marriage) 1. A relationship in which one person is married to two spouses, regardless of the sex of those spouses. 2. Legal In most Western countries, the crime of entering in one marriage while still legally married to another person; marriage fraud. Contrast monogamy; See related polygamy, polygyny, polyandry. See related Enoch Arden Act.

BIPOLY: Colloquial Of or related to a person who is both bisexual and polyamorous.

BI POLY SWITCH: Colloquial; sometimes humorous Of or related to a person who is bisexual and polyamorous and who is a BDSM «switch», capable of taking on a «dominant» or «submissive» role in sex. Commentary: A popular T-shirt reads "I'm a bi poly switch and I still won't sleep with you."

BISEXUAL: Of or related to sexual attraction to or sexual activity with more than one sex or gender; as, a bisexual person: a person who is sexually

attracted to or sexually active with partners of other sexes or genders.
http://robynochs.com/bisexual/

BLACK FEMINISM: See Womanism or
https://www.usatoday.com/story/news/2017/03/30/black-women-womanism-feminism/99514484/

BODY FLUID MONOGAMY: The practice of limiting any activity which involves the exchange of bodily fluids, including such activities as unprotected sexual intercourse, to only one partner. See also fluid bonding, condom contract. Usage: Originated in the BDSM community; becoming increasingly uncommon in the BDSM and poly communities.

BOSTON MARRIAGE: Archaic A term used primarily in the 19th century for a household of two unmarried women who were financially and romantically independent. Today, it is generally presumed that many such arrangements were lesbian relationships.

CANDAULISM: Sexual arousal from watching one's spouse have sex with or engage in sexual activity with another person. See related BDSM: «voyeurism»

CELLULAR FAMILY: A family of three or more adults (and optionally children) who live together or near one another, share responsibility for joint finances and/or domestic responsibilities, and consider themselves to be part of a single family. See related group marriage. Etymology: The term was coined by Deborah Anapol.

CHEATING: In a relationship, any activity which violates the rules or agreements of that relationship, whether tacit or explicit. Commentary: In traditional monoamorous relationships, any sexual activity with anyone outside that relationship is generally viewed as cheating. In a polyamorous or swinging relationship, sexual activity with people outside the relationship may or may not be seen as cheating, depending on the context of that sexual activity and whether or not it violates the agreements of the people in that relationship. Even in such relationships, most commonly sexual activity without the knowledge and explicit consent of the other members of the relationship is likely to be viewed as cheating. "Cheating is any violation of a trust." - from Dr. Shirley P. Glass, NOT just friends.

CHOICE FAMILY; also CHOSEN FAMILY: See intentional family.

CLOSED MARRIAGE: Any marriages where there is no emotional intimacy or sexuality outside the marriage; monogamous marriage. Contrast open marriage. Commentary: This is the most common form of marriage in most Western countries.

CLOSED GROUP MARRIAGE: A polyfidelitous relationship in which all the members consider themselves to be married. See related group marriage.

CLOSED-GROUP SWINGING: A form of swinging in which people will have multiple sexual partners within a specific group (as, for example, two couples who will swap partners), but will not have sex with people outside the group. A closed-group swinging relationship can look very similar to a polyfidelitous relationship from the outside; the primary difference between them often being the focus of the relationship (sexual vs. romantic) rather than the form of the relationship. See also friends-first swinging.

CLOSED RELATIONSHIP: Any romantic relationship, such as a conventional monogamous relationship or a polyfidelitous relationship, which specifically excludes the possibility of sexual or romantic connections outside that relationship.

CLOSED SWINGING: A practice in which a group of swingers will exchange partners and then have sex separately, usually in separate rooms; swinging without group sex.Contrast open swinging. Usage: Common in the swinging community; uncommon outside it.

CLUSTER MARRIAGE: A polyamorous relationship in which two or more married couples cohabitate and exchange partners. See group marriage; See related intentional family, co-spouse, co-husband, co-wife.

COLLARING/COLLARING CEREMONY: Collaring Ceremony/ Wedding (Ring) A collaring ceremony is a bonding ritual used by Dominants and submissives to not only solidify their relationship, but to be recognized by friends and by the community as a committed relationship (in BDSM relationships). (From Sir Orpheus Black's blog at askOrpheusBlack.blogspot.com)

COLLECTIVE: A collective is a group of entities that share or are motivated by at least one common issue or interest, or work together to achieve a common objective. - Wikipedia. A cooperative enterprise, group, or communal living arrangement, particularly in an urban setting. The term was appropriated in the 1960s by the Black Panther Party for its member residences (in opposition to 'commune,' which was seen in the Black community as predominantly white, middle-class, elitist, and agrarian). Ref: cited by historian Robyn C. Spencer (@RaceWomanist) in 'Communalism and the Black Panther Party in Oakland, California,' in the anthology, West of Eden: Communes and Utopia in Northern California, 2012.

COLONIST, also MISSIONARY, COLONIZER: A person from outside of a community who enters that community and attempts to replace the community's mores, language, icons, heroes, history, lineage, thought leaders, theoreticians, value systems, and philosophy with that person's own. As with the colonists and missionaries from sociology, they operate from a posture of assumed and comprehensive superiority. Ref: former Black Panther Party central committee member Simba Wiley Roberts, c. 1969.

COMET: [kom-it] Noun. 1. A person that passes through your life repeatedly who is intense and awesome, and when gone you are still in contact with that person in some way but they are not a continuous partner.

Example: Ana is excited to have her comet Fredrico visit because they have hot sex and a deep connection. This is despite him living in Granada Spain and focusing on his poetry, while Ana lives in Seattle with her primary.

I have found there is a hole in the poly lexicon. The term "play partner" doesn't fit non-casual partners. Play sounds trite. Some of these relationships can span years and even decades. Some are very deep, with a combination of intimacy, friendship, admiration, and shared history. Poly circles use the term "play and pause" which also doesn't fit many of my "comets" as I don't pause. Many I stay in touch with daily or weekly.

Some comets come by every 18 months when the schedules line up or, to continue the metaphor, when the stars align. I have even heard some use the term partner-partner. As in, "they are a partner but not like a partner-partner." This is an example of that awkward lack of a term for someone who is somewhere between fully in your life at all times and a casual play play partner, that you like, but don't have an ongoing connection with.

(The term 'comet' has been floating around for a while, but we somehow neglected to add it here. It seems to have appeared on Reddit on April 17, 2016, posted by Voleuse; shared with B&P by Quiana Perkins).

COMPERSION: A feeling of joy when a partner invests in and takes pleasure from another romantic or sexual relationship. Commentary: it is a positive emotional reaction to a lover's other relationship.

Also: The preeminent and wildly popular digital series about a black family discovering polyamory. The Enchant.TV project was written, produced, and directed by Jackie J. Stone, and stars Jammie Patton, Derrick LeMont Sanders, and ka'Ramuu Kush.

The term was coined by the Kerista Commune. Kerista Commune.

COMPLEX MARRIAGE: A doctrine which holds that all the male members of a particular group or community are, upon joining the group, married to all the female members, and all the female members are, upon joining the group, married to all the male members. This doctrine was established as part of the Oneida Community.

CONDOM CONTRACT; also CONDOM COMPACT, CONDOM COMMITMENT: A formal agreement within a relationship to confine exchange of bodily fluids and barrier-free sexual contact to the people in that relationship, each of whom has previously been screened for sexually transmitted diseases. Condom contracts may specify under what conditions a member of that group may exchange body fluids or have sexual contact without barriers with a new partner, or may specify that such contact is not permissible with any new partner.

CO-HABITATE; also, COHABITATE, COHABIT: To live together. Cohabitating: the state or practice of living together.

CO-HUSBAND: A man in a group marriage who shares a spouse in common with at least one other man in that group marriage. See also co-wife, co-spouse.

CO-PRIMARY: A person who is one of two or more primary partners in a polyamorous relationship, as Bob and Joe are my co-primaries. See also primary/secondary; See related secondary, tertiary.

CORPORATE MARRIAGE: A group marriage whose members register the union as a legal corporation, the terms of which spell out the financial entanglements and obligations of all the members.

CO-SPOUSE: A person in a group marriage who shares a spouse in common with another person in that group marriage. See also metamour, co-husband, co-wife.

CO-WIFE: A woman in a group marriage who shares a spouse in common with at least one other woman in that group marriage. See also co-husband, co-spouse.

COUPLE'S PRIVILEGE: "The presumption that socially sanctioned pair-bond relationships involving only two people (such as marriage, long-term boyfriend/girlfriend, or other forms of conventional intimate/life partnerships) are inherently more important, "real" and validthan other types of intimate, romantic or sexual relationships. Such primary couples (or partnerships that are clearly riding society's standard relationship escalator toward that goal) are widely presumed — even within many nonmonogamous communities — to warrant more recognition and support than other types of intimate relationships."
http://solopoly.net/2013/02/05/couple-privilege-having-it-doesnt-necessarily-make-you-an-asshole-but-it-can/

COVENANT MARRIAGE: Legal A marriage which includes a legally-binding clause in the marriage contract specifying that the couple can not divorce, or can not divorce easily. Commentary: Only a handful of states in the United States recognize covenant marriage provisions.

COWBOY/COWGIRL: Colloquial A person who engages in a relationship with a polyamorous individual with the intention of separating the individual from any other partners and bringing the individual into a monoamorous relationship. Also called a Cow (distillation of cowgirl/cowboy) and Siren (from mythology).

CROSS-COUPLE: Of or relating to activities between a member of one couple and a member of another couple; as, for example, cross-couple relationship, a relationship between one person who is part a couple and a second person who is part of another couple.

CUDDLE PARTY: Trademark A social gathering of adults which encourages consensual physical affection, such as cuddling, massage, and other forms of physical expression, but which forbids overt sexual activity or sexual stimulation. Commentary: The term "Cuddle Party" has been trademarked by Reid Mihalko, who owns a business organizing such parties in many cities, which are pay-for-attendance events.

CUPCAKE PARTY: Colloquial A gathering, usually involving only women and most often in a private residence, in which a group of people gather to explore their sexuality, discuss sex, experiment with sex toys, and so on. Etymology: The hostess of a cupcake party often provides refreshments, hence the name.

CYCLIC MONOGAMY: 1. Colloquial A relationship in which a person has several partners, and spends a set period of time with each partner, during which time he is sexually involved only with that partner. 2. Sociology Serial monogamy. Commentary: In the case of Def. 1, there have been several recorded cases in which a person, usually a man, has a job or life which requires regular travel, and maintains romantic partners in separate cities. Generally speaking, these partners do not know about one another, and each believes that the relationship is monogamous, though this is not always so; in some cases, some or all of the partners know of the existence of the other partners.

DADT (initialism): See don't ask, don't tell.

DAINTILIAN: An orientation where you are more attracted to Feminine Presenting Individuals, with any type of gender , mainly, but it takes longer to form/are extremely picky towards forming some form of attraction to those who are Masculine Presenting , with any type of gender. This attraction can be towards other gender identities and sexes (such as non-binary), but they are PRIMARILY/mainly attracted to feminine presenting individuals. @nebularomantic is the flag maker and term coiner. https://faesaridollie.tumblr.com/post/181879108528/daintilian-an-orientation-where-you-are-more/embed

DELTA: A triad relationship, specifically a triad in which each person is sexually and/or emotionally involved with all the other people. Etymology:

So named because the Greek letter Delta looks like a triangle. Usage: Seems to be primarily a regional expression in parts of the United States.

DEMISEXUAL: A demisexual is a person who does not experience sexual attraction unless they form an emotional connection. It's more commonly seen in, but by no means confined, to romantic relationships. The term demisexual comes from the orientation being "halfway between" sexual and asexual.Sep 18, 2018 wiki.asexuality.org/Demisexual

DEMOCRATIC FAMILY: Colloquial A family, typically a family practicing group marriage, in which all the adult partners are considered equal.

DOMINANT: See BDSM: «dominant».

DOMESTIC GROUP: Sociology A group of people, often but not always related by birth or marriage, who live together and practice joint control over the household and group property.

DON'T ASK, DON'T TELL (DADT): A relationship structure in which a person who is partnered has additional intimate relationships of which their partner requests to be kept uninformed, unexposed, and uninvolved.

DYAD: A relationship involving exactly two people. The most accepted form of romantic relationship in most Western countries is a monoamorous dyad. Contrast triad, quad; See related serial monogamy, amatonormativity.

ÉGOTISME À DEUX: (literally, French, egotism for two): A term used by members of the Oneida community for monogamy (monoamory).

ELECTIVE AFFINITY: Sociology A social system whereby people choose their own mates or spouses, as opposed to a society which practices arranged marriage.

EMOTIONAL FIDELITY: A belief or practice that emotional intimacy or love must be kept exclusive to a particular relationship, though sexual activity or other forms of physical intimacy may occur outside that relationship. Commentary: Some swingers practice emotional fidelity.

EMOTIONAL LIBERTARIANISM: A belief that every individual is entirely responsible for his or her own emotional responses, and that one person's behavior is never the "cause" of another person's emotion.

ENBYFRIEND: A common affectionate term for non-binary people is "enby," derived from the sound of the letters NB, the initials from Non-Binary. So, they would be your "enbyfriend." That is becoming popular in non-binary circles.

ENDOGAMY: A state or practice whereby individuals are permitted to marry only within a specific group, such as a religious or social group.

ENOCH ARDEN ACT; also, ENOCH ARDEN LAW: Legal Any law or statute permitting remarriage in a case where a person's spouse is missing and presumed dead, and exempting such a person from charges of bigamy should it later turn out that the missing spouse is still alive. Etymology: Enoch Arden was a character in a poem by Alfred Tennyson.

ESCALATOR: See Relationship Escalator.

ETHICAL SLUT: Colloquial A person who openly chooses to have multiple simultaneous sexual relationships in an ethical and responsible way, and who openly revels in that decision. See related responsible non-monogamy. Commentary: The term comes from the book The Ethical Slut, which advocates reclaiming the word "slut" from its derogatory meaning of a promiscuous woman.

ETHICAL SLUT, THE: A book (Dossie Easton and Catherine A. Liszt, Greenery Press, 1998, ISBN 1890159018) which outlines a framework for responsible non-monogamy and champions taking joy in ethical, safe promiscuity. Commentary: The Ethical Slut is not a book about polyamory per se; the primary focus is on creating relationships which are not sexually monogamous and are positive and healthy, but it does not focus exclusively on loving or emotional intimate relationships, and does not create frameworks for managing the emotional or romantic component of such relationships. Nevertheless, it is very popular in the polyamory community, and is very useful to many polyamorous people. The ideas described in The Ethical Slut are pertinent to and valuable in swinging relationships as well.

EXCLUSION JEALOUSY: Psychology A fear, which may be irrational, of being neglected or abandoned by a lover, particularly if that lover takes another partner or expresses sexual or romantic interest in another. Commentary: The term exclusion jealousy was coined by Ronald Mazer in the book The New Intimacy: Open-Ended Marriage and Alternative Lifestyles (Beacon Press, 1973, ISBN 0595001025).

EXCLUSIVE RELATIONSHIP: 1. A monoamorous relationship. 2. Any relationship which does not permit its partners to seek other romantic or sexual partners at will; as, for example, a polyfidelitous relationship.

ERE (Existing Relationship Energy), see ORE (Old/Original Relationship Energy):

EXOGAMY: Marriage to a partner outside of one's particular group, such as a religious or social group.

EXPANDED FAMILY: See intentional family.

FEAR OF ABANDONMENT: See autophobia.

FEAR OF REJECTION: also called Rejection Sensitive Dysphoria (RSD) - People who have RSD don't handle rejection well. They get very upset if they think someone has shunned or criticized them, even if that's not the case. Up to 99% of teens and adults with ADHD are more sensitive than usual to rejection. People who have the condition sometimes work hard to make everyone like and admire them. Or they might stop trying and stay out of any situation where they might get hurt. This social withdrawal can look like social phobia, which is a serious fear of being embarrassed in public.

RSD can affect relationships with family, friends, or a romantic partner. The belief that you're being rejected can turn into a self-fulfilling prophecy. When you act differently toward the person you think has rejected you, they may begin to do so for real. - from https://www.webmd.com/add-adhd/rejection-sensitive-dysphoria#1

FEMINISM: (from the French feminisme, late 19th century, meaning feminine) a spectrum of socio-political movements and ideologies that have a base goal to establish equal rights for all genders in the political, economic, and social spheres, by focusing on the minority group who did not have equal rights. Mainstream feminism, however, has been tainted by the historical focus on white middle to upper-class women and thus ignoring the intersection between all women's issue. In short, it is blinded by white privilege. - Shalyse Wright-Bethea

FISHING FLEET: Colloquial Originally, the wives of sailors at sea, who would socialize together and look for prospective lovers together. More generally, a group of women who will get together and seek out new sexual partners, typically without their partners' knowledge, while their partners are unavailable or away.

FLEXUOUS TRIAD: (also flex triad, flux triad) An actively fluid triad whose members may also domicile elsewhere or identify differently at varying times and/or in other spaces. Example: A, B, and C identify as a triad. They cohabit occasionally. When not all together, they may continue to identify as a triad, even when one of them is identified as part of another dynamic concomitantly. From Latin flectere. It can mean fluid, undulating, or 'to bend.' Spurred by an August 2021 conversation between Ron Young and Käto Cooks on the nature of some triads in the real world as not fixed constructions, but as amorphous interrelationships between people, realistically capable of impermanent flux.

FLUID BONDING: Of or related to practices which involve the exchange of bodily fluids, such as barrier-free sexual intercourse and BDSM: «blood play». See related condom contract.

FOUR-CORNERED MARRIAGE: A group marriage with exactly four adult members; usually but not always a group marriage with two men and two women. See related quad. Etymology: The term "four-cornered marriage" is often attributed to Robert Heinlein.

FRANKENPOLY: The concept of realizing a whole relationship experience, or garnering complete relationship needs, from the collected attributes of more than one partner. (Etymology: Unclear, but it seems to have been popularized in Franklin Veaux and Eve Rickert's More Than Two.)

FRATERNAL POLYANDRY: See adelphogamy.

FREE AGENT: Colloquial A person who practices polyamory in a way that tends to separate or isolate all of his or her romantic relationships from one another, treating each as a separate entity. A free agent often presents himself or herself as "single" or behaves in ways which are typically associated with the behavior of a single person even when he or she has romantic partners, and often does not consider the potential impact of new relationships upon existing relationships when deciding whether or not to pursue those new relationships.

FREE LOVE: The belief that sexual relationships should be unrestricted and disassociated from ideas of love, commitment, marriage, or obligation. Commentary: Many advocates of free love object to the concept of marriage altogether, as they see it as a way to impose constraints and obligation on sexuality. Etymology: The term free love is generally attributed to John Humphrey Noyes, founder of the Oneida Community, who later abandoned it in favor of complex marriage.

FREEMATE: A non-married partner in a group relationship. See related metamour, group marriage.

FRICTION PARTY: Colloquial; see cuddle party. Commentary: The term "friction party" is not trademarked; the term cuddle party is. Friction parties, unlike cuddle parties, are informal social gatherings that aren't typically run as a business, may not be open to general admission (that is, they may be private), and may or may not charge for access.

FRIENDS-FIRST SWINGING: A form of swinging in which the people involved do not engage in sexual activities with anonymous or random partners, but instead have sex outside an existing relationship only with other people who are already close friends. In this form of swinging, emotionally intimate bonds can and often do form among all the people involved; this kind of swinging can often look very similar to polyamory, the primary difference between them often being the focus of the relationship (sexual vs. romantic) rather than the form of the relationship. See also closed-group swinging. Commentary: Hollywood images of swing clubs and anonymous sex aside, friends-first swinging is arguably one of the most common forms of swinging.

FRIENDS WITH BENEFITS (FWB): A relationship in which two (or more) people establish a friendship which includes sex or sexual activity, but without romantic love and typically without the same type or degree of expectations or other practical or emotional entanglements that typically accompany romantic relationships.

FUCKBUDDY: Colloquial; vulgar See friends with benefits.

FWB (ACRONYM): See friends with benefits.

GEOGRAPHICAL NON-MONOGAMY: Any relationship or arrangement whose partners permit one another to have other sexual partners while they are physically apart, as for example a relationship in which one person takes a temporary position in another town or is assigned overseas for a time. Usually carries an implicit understanding that when the couple is physically together again, the relationship will become monogamous. See related hundred-mile rule.

GROUP MARRIAGE: A relationship in which three or more people consider themselves married to one another; in the polyamory community, most often a relationship involving more than one man and more than one woman, who may live together, share finances, raise children together, and otherwise share those responsibilities normally associated with marriage. A group marriage is not recognized by and has no legal standing within most Western countries, but may have symbolic or emotional value to the people involved. Many people who believe in group marriage may create civil contracts and other legally binding business arrangements which specify the type and extent of financial commitments within the marriage, or even form a legal corporation which defines the marriage. See related corporate marriage, cluster marriage, polygamy, polyandry, polygyny, troika.

HANDFASTING: A Pagan or Wiccan ceremony similar to marriage in the sense that it unites two people in a common bond, but dissimilar to a traditional Western marriage in that it does not necessarily convey sexual exclusivity and may not be intended to be permanent (some handfasting ceremonies last "for a year and a day," others for "as long as the love shall last"). A handfasting is not legally recognized as a marriage unless the person performing the handfasting is authorized to perform marriages in a particular jurisdiction (requirements for such authorization vary from place to place) and the other legal requirements of marriage are met. Commentary: Handfasting ceremonies are not directly related to polyamory; however, some people, particularly those involved with Wiccan or neo-Pagan spirituality or beliefs, may combine the two. While not all Pagans are polyamorous and not all polyamorous people are Pagan, there is enough overlap between the communities that some polyamorous people practice handfasting as an emotional or spiritual symbol of their relationships and commitment.

HARD SWINGER: A swinger who has sexual intercourse or engages in other sexual activity with other swingers outside of his or her existing relationship. Usage: Common in the swinging community, but uncommon in the polyamorous community. Contrast soft swinger.

HBB (Initialism): Colloquial; see hot bi babe.

HEINLEIN, ROBERT A. (1907-1988): An American science fiction author well-known in the polyamory community as an early advocate and outspoken champion of polyamory. Many of his novels, most notably the Hugo-award-winning Stranger in a Strange Land (Ace, 1961, ISBN 0441790348), feature polyamorous characters and relationships.

HINGE: Colloquial; see pivot.

HOBOSEXUAL: Noun. (plural hobosexuals) A person sexually attracted to "tramps" (as a paronomastic synonym of hobo). Punning on bum (as a synonym of hobo). A person of an unkempt appearance (antonymous with metrosexual). From www.yourdictionary.com/hobosexual

Also: a person who solicits, accepts, or engages in a relationship for the purpose of garnering housing; a homeless person whose hidden objective in a relationship is to have a place to stay. And from Sherrie Libra (Sherrie Brown): Also called 'homelesssexual.'

HOMOMISIA, HOMOMISIC: A strong dislike or hatred of homosexuals and homosexuality. Note: Distinct from homophobia, which is a fear of homosexuals or homosexuality. See https://diversitypride.org/misiaplege.html#:~:text=Homomisia%20%2F%20Homomisic,people%3B%20prejudice%20against%20gay%20people ; also https://www.thehofstrachronicle.com/category/editorials/2018/2/7/is-homophobia-outdated-the-root-of-the-problem, https://www.wholereason.com/2007/03/homomisia-and-islamomisia-not-phobia.html, and https://www.wordsense.eu/Citations:homomisia/

Usage: Those who treat gay people poorly and are anti-gay rights are often mislabeled as having a fear, homophobia, when they really have homomisia.

HOT BI BABE (HBB): Colloquial; often derogatory, condescending, or ironic A bisexual person, usually though not always female, who is willing to join an existing couple, often with the presumption that this person will date and become sexually involved with both members of that couple, and not demand anything or do anything which might cause problems or inconvenience to that couple. The term is often used to be dismissive of a couple seen to be only superficially polyamorous, as They're just looking for a hot bi babe. Such a person may be referred to as a "mythical hot bi babe." Some members of the polyamory community self-identify as hot bi babes as a form of tongue-in-cheek intentional irony.

HOTEP: Someone labeled as or self-identifying as a Hotep generally has beliefs as follows (though there are always exceptions, like in everything else):

- black nationalist

- believe everything/most positive things done were done by black ppl and white ppl later lied about it

- ancient Egypt is the root/center of black history and culture (contrast this to Black Hebrew Israelites who believe biblical Jews were black and Egypt was still the bad guy)

- heavy sense of patriarchy. The man is king. The woman is queen. The man is in charge, the woman is subordinate.

- OPP or harem relationship rules

- homophobia

- misogyny

- toxic masculinity

- strong emphasis on building, whether it be communities, 'empires', etc

You'll notice that some of the attributes aren't inherently bad (like building communities and such). The problem it often triggers with many (often younger members like me) is that the 'good' things are almost always paired with the heavily toxic things like homophobia/misogyny/etc. And it's not uncommon for some ppl to take an idea like building and make ppl/women into objects towards that end, which is bad. - Marcus Pyles, Sep 5 , 2018 in a thread in the Facebook group, Black & Poly.

Writing eloquently for The Root, Damon Young defined a hotep as "a person who's either a clueless parody of Afrocentricity" or "loudly, conspicuously and obnoxiously pro-black but anti-progress." May 8, 2018

"Hotep" is an Egyptian word that means "at peace." It's basically the Egyptian "What's good?" Over the past several decades, the word has also been utilized quite frequently by black Americans who happen to be more Afrocentric. Let me put it this way: If you happen to attend a Juneteenth festival this year and collect business cards from vendors there, at least 17 percent of them will have "Hotep" written somewhere on them. - The Root, Mar 5, 2016 Full article here: https://www.theroot.com/hotep-explained-1790854506

HOTWIFE; also, HOT WIFE: Colloquial A married woman who takes male lovers outside the marriage, often in the context of swinging or BDSM: «cuckoldry»

HUNDRED-MILE RULE: Colloquial An arrangement within a nominally monogamous marriage or relationship, particularly a marriage in which one of the partners travels a great deal or is often away from home for extended periods of time, which says that sexual dalliances which occur during the course of these travels or over a certain distance from the home don't "really" count and hence aren't cheating. See related don't ask, don't tell.

INTENTIONAL COMMUNITY: A residential community made up of people who share a common set of ideas, principles, or goals, and deliberately set out to create a planned community which reflects those ideas and goals. Intentional communities need not be polyamorous; there are intentional communities built around common religious, philosophical, or economic ideas, for example. Some polyamorous families create intentional communities with the idea of deliberately constructing a community built around non-monogamous relationship structures.

INTENTIONAL FAMILY: A family made up of people who have consciously and deliberately chosen to consider one another as a single family, as opposed to family that is the result of birth or marriage (i.e., family in law). See related cluster marriage, polyamory, group marriage. Usage: Most often used to describe a family of three or more adults.

INTERSECTIONALITY: coined in the 1980s by law professor Kimberlé Crenshaw – the theory of how different types of discrimination interact; also intersectionality theory – the study of how different power structures interact in the lives of minorities, specifically black women, - how feminist and anti-racist campaigns have left "women of colour invisible in plain sight." Reference:

 http://www.newstatesman.com/lifestyle/2014/04/kimberl-crenshaw-intersectionality-i-wanted-come-everyday-metaphor-anyone-could

INTIMATE NETWORK: Colloquial The sum total of a person's partners, those partners' partners, and so on. Usage: The term "intimate network" is most often used to describe the set of romantic and sexual relationships and friendships involved in a polyamorous relationship structure that is not closed; that is, the term intimate network is not often used to describe a polyfidelitous relationship or a closed group marriage, though it can be. The term is also sometimes used in a way that includes people who are close friends, but are not necessarily romantically or sexually involved, with a person or that person's partners.

JEALOUSY: A feeling of anger or bitterness that arises when something we already possess or feel we possess (usually a special relationship) is threatened or potentially claimed by another person or persons. Distinct from envy, which is when we desire attributes of others for ourselves, although in popular culture, the two are used interchangeably.

A subset of this is Perception Jealousy, coined by Lavitaloca Sawyers in 2018 during a livecast with Kimchi Cuddles author Tikva Wolf: "When... jealous of other people's perception of my partner's relationship with their partner." Example described here:
https://www.facebook.com/lavitalocasawyers/videos/668640846840370/Uzpf STIzOTg4NjkxMjgzMTA2MToxMTU4NjUyNzE0Mjg3ODA1/

For the difference between jealousy and envy, see
https://www.psychologytoday.com/us/blog/joy-and-pain/201401/what-is-the-difference-between-envy-and-jealousy Graphic thanks to Chaneè Jackson Kendall."

KERISTA COMMUNE: An experiment in polyamorous living in San Francisco, which was founded in 1971 and broke up in 1991. The Kerista

Commune was founded on the ideas of group marriage, shared economic resources, and intentional community. The commune was organized into "clusters," each of which was typically made up of between four and fifteen people and each of which functioned as a single polyfidelitous group. The Kerista Commune championed group control of individual responsibility, even going so far in some cases as to make group decisions about individual members' vocations, and assigning members to sleeping partners on a rotating schedule. The commune disbanded following very serious internal rifts in the early 1990s. Commentary: The Kerista Commune was an early advocate of polyamory, coining terms now common in the polyamorous community such as compersion and polyfidelity. The group eventually failed for a number of reasons, among them personality conflicts within the group, problems with financial management, an emphasis on fixed and inflexible sleeping schedules, and hostile attitudes toward bisexuality and homosexuality on the part of some members.

KEY CLUB: Colloquial; see swing club (Def. 2).

KEY PARTY: A specific type of play party (Def. 1), usually attended by couples, in which each male deposits his keys into a container as he arrives. As the guests leave, each female draws a set of keys at random from the container, then goes home with the male to which they belong that night. Usage: A key party is typically a swinger event.

KITCHEN TABLE POLYAMORY: Kitchen Table Polyamory is a new term even in poly circles. It refers to poly relationships where everyone in the polycule is comfortable sitting together at the kitchen table with a cup of coffee. Folks who prefer kitchen table polyamory want to know their metamours and be friends with them. They may want their kids and their metamour's kids to spend time together, or their metamour's other partners to be comfortable calling them up to plan a surprise party together. (Definition taken from http://PolyamoryonPurpose.com, August 4, 2016)

KYRIARCHY: pronounced /ˈkaɪriɑːrki/, is a social system or set of connecting social systems built around domination, oppression, and submission. The word was coined by Elisabeth Schüssler Fiorenza in 1992 to describe her theory of interconnected, interacting, and self-extending systems of domination and submission, in which a single individual might be oppressed in some relationships and <u>privileged</u> in others. It is an <u>intersectional</u> extension of the idea of <u>patriarchy</u> beyond gender.[1] Kyriarchy encompasses <u>sexism</u>, <u>racism</u>, <u>speciesism</u>, <u>homophobia</u>, <u>classism</u>, <u>economic injustice</u>, <u>colonialism</u>, <u>militarism</u>, <u>ethnocentrism</u>, <u>anthropocentrism</u>, and other forms of dominating hierarchies in which the subordination of one person or group to another is internalized and institutionalized. from Wikipedia, but offered by Son of Baldwin (on Facebook).

LANGDON CHART: A chart which indicates a person's current and past sexual partners, and all their partners' current and past sexual partners, and so on. Etymology: Coined by Kevin Langdon in the mid-1960s. See <u>http://fancyclopedia.org/langdon-chart</u>

LAT: An acronym for Living Apart Together, is a relatively new relationship model in the eyes of Statistics Canada. The 2011 General Social Survey estimated that <u>1.9 million Canadians</u> were couples living apart together. These are people who are in committed relationships but who choose to live in different homes, whether that's in the same city or a different one. Article: <u>https://globalnews.ca/news/4318749/living-apart-together-</u><u>couples/?fbclid=IwAR152f53bB5SsNOMUBwJ-</u><u>mZuDBlNtEsw6un1RGbBrBA3b6GJYb-_UsV4h28</u>

LDR (initialism): See long-distance relationship.

LESBIAN SHEEPITUDE: Colloquial A term used to describe a situation where one person has a romantic or sexual interest in another person, which may be reciprocated, but neither of them indicates this interest or makes the first move. Etymology: The colloquialism comes from the behavior of sheep; a female ewe indicates sexual interest and receptiveness by standing still, so two hypothetical lesbian sheep would indicate their sexual receptivity by each standing still, and no mating would take place. Commentary: This expression is often heard on the UseNet newsgroup alt. polyamory.

LEVIRATIC MARRIAGE: Sociology A system by which when a man dies, his brother marries his widow.

LEVIRATIC POLYANDRY: Sociology Adelphogamy.

LIFE PARTNER: A partner, usually a romantic and sexual partner, with whom one has the intent of a long-lasted and intertwined committed relationship. Commentary: A life partner need not necessarily be a spouse, though most often a spouse is a life partner. In some cases, someone may consider a partner's partner to be a life partner even though there is no direct sexual or romantic relationship with that person.

LIFESTYLE: noun (from Dictionary.com); distinct from loves tyle

1. the way in which a person or group lives. "the benefits of a healthy lifestyle" synonyms: way of life, way of living, life, situation, fate, lot; More

2. denoting advertising or products designed to appeal to a consumer by association with a desirable lifestyle. modifier noun: lifestyle; modifier noun: life-style

LIMERENCE: A strong desire for, longing for, or preoccupation with another person, accompanied by a sometimes overwhelming desire for reciprocation. Limerence may be accompanied by idealization of the person so desired. Etymology: The term limerence was coined by Dr. Dorothy Tennov, who described it in her book Love and Limerence: The Experience of Being in Love (Scarborough House, 1979, ISBN 0812862864). Commentary: Limerence is distinct from new relationship energy in that it is more akin to what people commonly call a "crush," and may not be associated with a relationship at all. Some researchers have linked limerence to quantifiable physiological processes in the brain, particularly to depressed levels of the neurotransmitter serotonin. Some people in the polyamory community use the word limerence as a synonym for new relationship energy, though this usage is not technically correct.

LINE MARRIAGE; also, LINE FAMILY: A specific form of group marriage in which younger partners are added to the relationship as older partners age; in theory, such a relationship would eventually reach equilibrium, adding new partners as existing partners die. Etymology: The term (and the idea behind it) was coined by science fiction writer Robert A. Heinlein.

LINK:(n) an intimate connection with another person. Connections may be romantic, aromantic, sexual, asexual, platonic, kinky, or take other forms of intimacy. Connections can last a few hours or a life time. The number and nature of connections are determined only by the individuals who are connected. Source: https://medium.com/postmodern-woman/finally-that-integrated-term-for-non-monogamy-you-never-knew-you-needed-aac9e066fdc7

 Example: "I prefer having one stable long term link and lots of fun and exciting short term links. My friend Jen wants to find several people to link with for long term."

LONG-DISTANCE RELATIONSHIP (LDR): A relationship in which the people involved do not live together, and are separated by great distances; as, for example partners who live in different cities, in different states, or even in different countries.

LOVER-IN-LAW: Colloquial 1. A partner of one's partner; metamour. 2. The biological family of one's partner. Commentary: In the sense of Def. 1, most often applied to a metamour with whom one has a close relationship.

LOVE TRIANGLE: 1. See triad. 2. In contemporary American vernacular outside of the poly community, a relationship in which two people both love a third; in this usage, the assumption is that each of the two is competing for the undivided affections of the third, and that the third is being placed in a position where he or she is expected to choose one of the two competing partners.

LOVE QUADRANGLE: See quad.

LOVESTYLE: Type of intimate relationship, sexual and/or romantic; 'lovestyle' is used routinely in the Black & Poly (tm) community.
 See relationship orientation. Usage: Most common in New Age or tantra communities, according to the More Than Two glossary.

LOVING MORE: A magazine (PEP Publishing; ISSN 1523-5858) and organization dedicated to polyamory. The organization which publishes Loving More also sponsors a series of annual conventions by the same name.

MANSPLAIN: A portmanteau of man and the informal 'splain' that occurs when a person explains a thing from a dominant perspective possessed of cluelessness, arrogance and condescension:

1. (of a man) to comment on or explain something to a woman in a condescending, overconfident, and often inaccurate or oversimplified manner: He mansplained to her about female friendships.

2. to comment on or explain something to someone in such a way: I know some women who are guilty of mansplaining. Reference: Dictionary.com and https://www.guernicamag.com/rebecca-solnit-men-explain-things-to-me/ from where comes this fragment: "… I hasten to add that the essay makes it clear mansplaining is not a universal flaw of the gender, just the intersection between overconfidence and cluelessness where some portion of that gender gets stuck."

MARIAGE Á TROIS: (Literally, French, marriage of three) A marriage involving exactly three people, in which one person is married to two partners. See related triad, vee. Usage: Most commonly used of situations in which one man is married to two women.

MARRIAGE: A relationship, most commonly between one man and one woman in Western countries, which is sanctioned by the State and/or by a religious institution and which confers upon its members certain social and economic conditions, typically including rights of joint property ownership, rights of inheritance and of decision-making in legal and medical matters, and certain legal rights and responsibilities concerning mutual child rearing. These rights and responsibilities have varied over time and today vary from place to place, but common to all of them is the expectation that people who are married are in a legally recognized, financially entwined, committed relationship which is not trivial to separate. Traditionally, marriages in most Western countries carry with them expectations of sexual and emotional monogamy. See related closed marriage, open marriage, group marriage, polygamy, polygyny,polyandry. Commentary: Increasingly, Western countries are being forced to grapple with the issue of same-sex partnerships being officially recognized as marriages, both because gays and lesbians want the social status conferred by marriage and because gays and lesbians want the legal rights so conferred, particularly with regard to economic matters such as inheritance and joint property ownership, practical matters such as insurance and the right to make medical decisions on behalf of an incapacitated partner, and so on. Many people also feel that these legal rights and responsibilities do not have to be limited to exactly two people, and that partnerships involving more than two people are entitled to equal treatment under the law as well.

MASCULINE OF CENTER: see MoC.

MEGASEXUAL: Megasexuals are characterized as individuals who lack emotional connection toward any person or persons unless they first form a strong sexual connection with someone. The level of sexual connection it takes for an emotional bond to form is often dependent on the initial attraction to the person. It is an orientation that is not chosen but often discouraged due to sex-negative attitudes. Coined by Dr. Liz Powell and The Frisky Fairy during Atlanta Poly Weekend, 2015. More here: http://friskyfairy.com/wp/blog/2018/03/15/megasexuality-the-identity-of-a-slut/ (Thanks to Marcus Pyles for the introduction)

MÈNAGE Á TROIS: (Literally, French, house of three) 1. Sexual activity involving three people. 2. See triad. Commentary: In the sense of Def. 2, usually applied to a triad in which all three people involved live together.

METAMOUR: (Literally, meta with; about + amor love): The partner of one's partner, with whom one does not share a direct sexual or loving relationship. See related vee.

METAPARENT: Also Metamom/Metadad. formal, coined by Black & Poly founder Ron Young. A person acting as a parent who is in a Polyamorous union or relationship with one's parent to whom one is not blood-related (Similar to a stepparent). Example: // "Who's coming to pick you up after school Javier? Your mom or dad?". "Neither... My metaparent lives nearby so..."

METROSEXUAL: Metrosexual is a portmanteau of metropolitan and heterosexual, coined in 1994 describing a man who is especially meticulous about his grooming and appearance, typically spending a significant amount of time and money on shopping as part of this. - Wikipedia. There is also this: a usually urban heterosexual male given to enhancing his personal appearance by fastidious grooming, beauty treatments, and fashionable clothes. . - https://www.merriam-webster.com/dictionary/metrosexual

MISSIONARY, also COLONIST, COLONIZER: A person from outside of a community who enters that community and attempts to replace the community's mores, language, icons, heroes, history, lineage, thought leaders, theoreticians, value systems, and philosophy with that person's own. As with the colonists and missionaries from sociology, they operate from a posture of assumed and comprehensive superiority. Ref: former Black Panther Party central committee member Simba Wiley Roberts, c. 1969.

MoC (Masculine of Center): Masculine of Center (MoC) is a term, coined by B. Cole of the Brown Boi Project, that recognizes the breadth and depth of identity for lesbian/queer/ womyn who tilt toward the masculine side of the gender scale and includes a wide range of identities such as butch, stud, aggressive/AG, dom, macha, tomboi, trans-masculine, etc. ...Jun 13, 2011 from www.butchvoices.com/faqs/

MONOAMORY; also MONAMORY: (Literally, mono one + amor love): The state or practice of loving only one person at a time. Contrast polyamory; See also monogamy. Commentary: The word monoamory was coined as a response to the fact that the word monogamy literally means "one marriage;" technically speaking, a monogamous person, according to the word's roots, should be a person with only one spouse, regardless of the number of other romantic or sexual partners that person has. In practice, it means essentially the same thing as monogamy, though it is sometimes applied to a person who self-identifies as monogamous but is involved in a romantic relationship with a person who self-defines as polyamorous.

MONOGAMISH: Colloquial A relationship which is not necessarily sexually fidelitous, but that differs from polyamory in that the outside sexual relationships are seen as primarily sexual rather than romantic, without necessarily having any expectation of continuity, and are viewed as enhancing the primary couple. See related open marriage. Etymology: The term was coined by columnist Dan Savage to describe committed relationships that still allow some "outside" sexual dalliances.

MONOGAMY: (Literally, mono one + gamos marriage) Formally, the state or practice of having only one wedded spouse. Informally, the state or practice of having only one wedded spouse at a time, or more generally, having only one sexual partner or only one romantic relationship at a time. Monogamous: of or related to the practice of monogamy, as in monogamous relationship: a relationship permitting one and only one romantic or sexual partner. Also see Monoamory. Contrast polyamory, polygamy, polygyny, polyandry; See related closed marriage, serial monogamy.

MONO/POLY: Colloquial; see poly/mono.

MULTILATERAL MARRIAGE: See group marriage.

MOST SIGNIFICANT OTHER (MSO): A person's primary partner in a hierarchical primary/secondary relationship.

MSO (initialism): See most significant other. MULTILATERAL SEXUALITY: See responsible non-monogamy. Usage: Most common in the swinging community. N: Colloquial A polyamorous relationship involving four people, generally two couples where one member of one couple is also involved sexually and/or romantically with one member of the other couple. See also quad; See related triad, vee.

MULTI-LINKING: (n) from multi (many) + linking (connecting, relating) Source: https://medium.com/postmodern-woman/finally-that-integrated-term-for-non-monogamy-you-never-knew-you-needed-aac9e066fdc7 the personal quality or practice of co-creating or wanting to co-create intimate connections with multiple people. Connections may be romantic, aromantic, sexual, asexual, platonic, kinky, or take other forms of intimacy. Connections can last a few hours or a lifetime. The nature of connections are determined only by the individuals who are connected.
 Example: "I prefer multi-linking to monogamy. I like to have lots of different relationships and intimacies."

Multi-link: (v) to intimately connect with multiple people. Connections may be romantic, aromantic, sexual, asexual, platonic, kinky, or take other forms of intimacy. Connections can last a few hours or a life time. The number and nature of connections are determined only by the individuals who are connected.
 Example: "I multi-link. Right now I'm partners with Dan, nesting with Gloria and sub to Jesse. There are also several people I don't have defined links with, but who are part of my chosen family."

Link: (n) an intimate connection with another person. Connections may be romantic, aromantic, sexual, asexual, platonic, kinky, or take other forms of intimacy. Connections can last a few hours or a life time. The number and nature of connections are determined only by the individuals who are connected.

 Example: "I prefer having one stable long term link and lots of fun and exciting short term links. My friend Jen wants to find several people to link with for long term."

NEOLOGISM: A newly coined (invented or constructed) word or phrase. Most don't appear in dictionaries until popular usage is established.

NESTING PARTNER: A "nesting partner" is someone you cohabit intimately with, but with whom you do not engage in common "relationship escalator" behaviors (progression to marriage, blending finances, identifying as a "couple," shared-bedroom cohabitation, etc.), poly-hierarchy or couple-centrism. It's a way of indicating a cohabiting partnership, while also indicating that you do not engage in constructs that are often assumed of cohabiting lovers/partners. (ref: Bhramari Dasi)

NEW RELATIONSHIP ENERGY (NRE): Conterminous with Honeymoon Effect. A strong, almost giddy feeling of excitement and infatuation common in the beginning of any new romantic relationship. While similar in some ways to limerence, new relationship energy is distinct in that it often follows the beginning of a relationship (as opposed to desire for a relationship), and can last as long as several years. Contrast old/existing relationship energy. Commentary: Some researchers believe that new relationship energy is the result of the hormones oxytocin and vasopressin, which are released by the brain during the start of a new relationship and after a mother gives birth and are believed to have a role in emotional bonding and in the feelings of happiness and well-being that often accompany the start of a new relationship. Etymology, mid-1980s: http://aphroweb.net/nre_origin.htm

NOETISEXUAL: (noun) "Noetisexual — It's a mental attraction rather than a purely "intellectual" one. It's loving the shape of their mental landscape and wanting to explore it. It's falling in love with the way they think, their unique mental make up. It's loving their creativity, their ingenuity, their silliness, their humor, their emotional intelligence, the way they use words, or the way they make mental space for you in their minds, and more.

"It's being attracted to the way their minds work — not how their brain functions — rather than simply one ill-defined facet of it. Noeti can serve as a prefix in itself: noetisexual, noetiromantic, noetisensual, etc. Noetilinking,the general experience, is not a sexuality per se; it can be a type of attraction like sensual or emotional are types." - Michon Neal, from https://medium.com/@neal_michon/an-alternative-to-sapiosexual-671dc1bdf86a

NONEXCLUSIVE MONOGAMY: Of or related to any marriage involving exactly two people, whereby each of the two is permitted to have sex with others outside the relationship but may not marry (or in some cases conduct emotionally intimate relationships) outside the relationship. Contrast group marriage. Commentary: the word monogamy in nonexclusive monogamy is used in the formal sense of "one marriage," rather than in the general sense of "one sexual partner."

NRE (initialism): See new relationship energy.

NRE JUNKIE: Colloquial; usually derogatory A term sometimes applied, often dismissively, to a person who starts many new relationships in rapid succession but does not seem to maintain relationships for very long. Such a person may appear to seek out the euphoria and intense emotion associated with new relationship energy over the maintenance of a long-term relationship. Commentary: Some psychologists and psychiatrists believe that the intensity and euphoria associated with new relationship energy can be psychologically addictive; in the psychiatric community, the term "love addiction" is sometimes used to describe this behavior.

NUCLEAR FAMILY: A family consisting of one man and one woman, married to one another, and their children. In some religious and social groups, this structure is idealized as the only "right" form of family, though historically it has never been the dominant family structure in Western history.

OLD RELATIONSHIP ENERGY (ORE), also Existing Relationship Energy (ERE) : The feeling of comfort, security, and stability often associated with a long-standing romantic relationship. Contrast new relationship energy.

OMNIGAMY: 1. Group marriage. 2. Of or relating to having multiple spouses of both sexes. 3. Complex marriage. In the sense of Def. 2, See related bisexual.

OMNISEXUAL: (literally, all sexes) bisexual, pansexual. Usage: In some communities, particularly some parts of the lesbian and gay community, antipathy toward or hostility to people who self-identify as bisexual has become common. The term omnisexual has started to become popular as a synonym for bisexual but without the negative connotations of the word.

ONEIDA COMMUNITY: A religious intentional community founded in New York in 1848 by John Humphrey Noyes. Noyes founded a branch of Christianity called "Christian Perfectionism," a doctrine which holds that it is possible for a Christian to reach a state of sinlessness and moral perfection before God. The Oneida Community was created as a deliberately and intentionally Christian group, led by Noyes and championing this doctrine of Christian Perfectionism. One of the more notable features of the Oneida Community was the idea that all male members of the community were married to all female members of the community, and vice-versa, an arrangement Noyes termed complex marriage. Another interesting feature of the Oneida Community was its belief that men should learn to control the process of ejaculation during sexual intercourse; this practice was used as a method of birth control within the community. The Oneida Community disbanded in 1881, by which time it had grown to 306 members.

ONE PENIS POLICY, or OPP: An arrangement within a polyamorous relationship in which a man is allowed to have multiple female partners, each of whom is allowed to have sex with other women but forbidden to have any other male partners. Commentary: Its hypothetical opposite, a "one vagina policy" in which a woman has a group of male partners who are each forbidden to have other female lovers, seems so rare as to be theoretical.

OPEN MARRIAGE: Any marriage whose structures or arrangements permit one or both of the members involved to have outside sexual relationships, outside romantic relationships, or both. The term open marriage is a catchall for marriages which are not emotionally or sexually monogamous; and may include such activities as polyamory or swinging. Contrast closed marriage; See related group marriage. Commentary: The term "open marriage" is sometimes used as a synonym for polyamory, though this is not necessarily the case; some relationships may be open but not polyamorous (as in some swinging relationships which explicitly ban emotional entanglement with anyone outside the relationship), and some relationships may be polyamorous but not open (as in polyfidelitious relationships).

OPEN NETWORK: A relationship structure in which the people involved are free to add new partners as they choose. Contrast polyfidelity. Commentary: This is a very common form for polyamorous relationships.

OPEN RELATIONSHIP: 1. Any relationship that is not sexually monogamous. 2. Any relationship that permits "outside" sexual entanglements, but not loving or romantic relationships. Commentary: Some folks use the term open relationship as a synonym for polyamory. To other people, the term excludes polyamory, and is used specifically to describe relationships which are sexually non-monogamous but which still expect that the people involved will not fall in love or engage in romantic relationships outside the couple, as for example with many swinging relationships. It's important to be careful when using this term, as it may carry very different connotations for different people.

OPEN SWINGING: A practice in which a group of swingers will exchange partners and then have sex together in the same room; sometimes but not always assumes group sex. Contrast closed swinging. Usage: Common in the swinging community; uncommon outside it.

ORE (initialism): See old relationship energy.

ORGANIC RELATIONSHIP: A relationship that is not forced, contrived, or manipulated; without external influences or direction. Other perspectives: https://iammeganambers.com/2015/11/30/organic-relationships-and-love-affairs/

https://www.yourtango.com/experts/jason-hairston/organic-relationship

https://www.mamasaysnamaste.com/organic-relationships/

https://www.selfgrowth.com/articles/organic-relationship-building-trust-the-wisdom-of-ripeness

OTHER SIGNIFICANT OTHER (OSO): 1. A partner's other partner; metamour. 2. A person's partner, sometimes but not always a non-primary or non-spouse partner; as, Bob is my husband, and Joe is my other significant other.

OSO (initialism): See other significant other.

OPP (initialism): See one penis policy.

OTTER: A cohabiting individual (culled from an episode entitled, Monogamy, on the Netflix series, "explained.") Also see Nesting Partner(s).

OXYTOCIN: A naturally-occuring hormone produced in the hypothalamus and secreted from the pituitary gland. Oxytocin is produced both by men and women, and in women is known to play a role in uterine contraction during childbirth and in milk production. Production of this hormone increases during the early stages of a new relationship and during sex, and it is believed to be partly responsible for mediating the processes involved in emotional intimacy. New relationship energy is thought to be a result in part of oxytocin production. See related vasopressin.

PANAMORY: Of or relating to romantic or sexual love with partners of many sexes, sexual orientations, gender identities, and/or relationship orientations. Panamorous, of or relating to one who identifies as a person capable of romantic or sexual love with many kinds of partners regardless of their sex, sexual orientation, or gender identity.

PANSEXUAL: See BDSM: «PANSEXUAL». Pansexuality, or omnisexuality, is the sexual, romantic or emotional attraction towards people regardless of their sex or gender identity. Pansexual people may refer to themselves as gender-blind, asserting that gender and sex are not determining factors in their romantic or sexual attraction to others. - Wikipedia. Also see: https://www.independent.co.uk/life-style/love-sex/pansexuality-definition-explained-bisexuality-difference-meaning-preferences-janelle-monae-a8325171.html

https://www.minus18.org.au/index.php/resources/sexuality-info/item/647-bisexual-vs-pansexual

https://www.seventeen.com/love/a20084651/pansexual-vs-bisexual-definition-difference/

https://www.psychologytoday.com/us/blog/sex-sexuality-and-romance/201711/the-truth-about-pansexuality

PARALLEL POLYAMORY: is a companion term to kitchen table polyamory. It refers to poly relationships where the relationships run in parallel and don't interact. I'm in a relationship with you, and you are in a relationship with your other partner, but the two of us aren't friends and may never meet. Our two separate relationships progress without connecting to each other. (From http://PolyamoryonPurpose.com, August 4, 2016)

PARAMOUR: (literally, par way + amor love; by way of love) 1. A married person's outside lover. 2. A mistress--the unmarried female lover of a married man. 3. A nonmarried member of a polyamorous relationship. See related other significant other.

PERSON OF COLOR, (plural: PEOPLE OF COLOR), PoC: a person who is not white or of European heritage; a term used mainly in the United States to describe any person who is not white. From Wikipedia: the term encompasses all non-white people, emphasizing common experiences of systemic racism. See also:

https://www.npr.org/sections/codeswitch/2014/03/30/295931070/the-journey-from-colored-to-minorities-to-people-of-color

https://www.sapiens.org/column/race/people-of-color/

https://www.crisis-center.org/diversity/people-of-color/

PISTANTHROPHOBIA: The fear of trusting people due to bad experiences with prior lovers. Dec 12, 2013 https://goodmenproject.com/featured-content/kt-been-through-a-messy-break-up-then-you-may-suffer-from-pistanthrophobia/

PIVOT: Colloquial In a vee relationship, the person who has two partners.

PLATONIC RELATIONSHIP: A close, emotionally intimate relationship in which there is no sex or physical intimacy.

PLURAL MARRIAGE: See polygamy.

POLY: Colloquial Of or related to polyamory; as, a poly relationship, a poly person.

POLYAGONY: A term coined by Jillian Deri in her book, Love's Refraction (link is external), based on findings from her study of jealousy and compersion in queer women's polyamorous relationships. "Deri coined the term polyagony to describe the special jealous pain that can plague some people in polyamorous relationships." - Dr. Elisabeth Sheff.

POLYAMORY: (Literally, poly many + amor love) The state, potential, or practice of maintaining multiple intimate or romantic relationships simultaneously, with the full knowledge of all the people involved (no secrets, no lies). Polyamorous: of or related to the practice of polyamory, as in polyamorous relationship: a relationship involving more than two people, or open to involvement by more than two people; polyamorous person: a person who prefers or is open to intimate or romantic relationships with more than one partner simultaneously. Contrast monogamy; See related polyfidelity, triad, quad, vee, N,polygamy, polygyny, polyandry, swinging, monogamy. Commentary: There is some debate over the origin of the word.

The Oxford English Dictionary attributes the word to Jennifer Wesp, who founded the newsgroup alt. polyamory in 1992. The term polyamorous is often attributed to Morning Glory Zell, who used it to describe situations in which a person engages in multiple loving, committed relationships simultaneously in the essay "A Bouquet of Lovers." It appears that both people coined the term independently and simultaneously.

Polyamory is not necessarily related directly to marriage or to polygamy; a person may have no spouse or only one spouse and still be polyamorous. Many people use the term "polyamory" to describe only those relationships in which a person has multiple loving partners; some people have extended the term to include relationships in which a person has multiple sexual partners regardless of the emotional component or degree of commitment between them, though this meaning was not a part of Morning Glory Zell's original intent for the word.

In 1992, when the editors of the Oxford English Dictionary contacted Morning Glory Zell to ask for a formal definition and background of the word, part of her response was "The two essential ingredients of the concept of "polyamory" are "more than one" and "loving." That is, it is expected that the people in such relationships have a loving emotional bond, are involved in each other's lives multi-dimensionally, and care for each other. This term is not intended to apply to merely casual recreational sex, anonymous orgies, one-night stands, pick-ups, prostitution, "cheating," serial monogamy, or the popular definition of swinging as "mate-swapping" parties."

POLYANDRY: (Literally, poly many + andros man) The state or practice of having multiple wedded husbands at the same time. Contrast monogamy; see related polygamy, polygyny, bigamy.

POLYCULE: A polycule, in the <u>polyamory</u> and <u>BDSM</u> communities, is a word that refers to all the people in a network of non-<u>monogamous</u> relationships (not being committed to one person at a time). Polycule can also refer to diagrams of these relationship networks. (from <u>https://www.dictionary.com/e/gender-sexuality/polycule/</u>)

POLY FAMILY: Colloquial 1. A set of polyamorous people who live together and identify as part of the same family. 2. A polyamorous group whose members consider one another to be family, regardless of whether or not they share a home.

POLYFI: Colloquial; see polyfidelity.

POLYFIDELITY: (Literally, poly many + fidelitas faithfulness) A romantic or sexual relationship which involves more than two people, but which does not permit the members of that relationship to seek additional partners outside the relationship, at least without the approval and consent of all the existing members. Some polyfidelitous relationships may have a mechanism which permits adding new members to the relationship with mutual agreement and consent of the existing members; others may not permit any new members under any circumstances. Etymology: The term polyfidelity was coined by the Kerista Commune.

POLYFUCKERY: Colloquial; vulgar; often derogatory A coarse term sometimes used to describe people who call themselves "polyamorous" while engaging in a large number of sexual relationships which are short-lived or not emotionally intimate; as Bob practices polyfuckery. Almost always indicates derision of the activity or person so named. Usage: Almost always used only of people who self-describe as 'polyamorous;' not used to describe, for example, people who identify as swingers. See related polysexual.

POLYGAMY: (Literally, poly many + gamos marriage) The state or practice of having multiple wedded spouses at the same time, regardless of the sex of those spouses. Contrast monogamy; See related polyandry, polygyny, bigamy. Commentary: Polygyny is the most common form of polygamy in most societies which permit multiple spouses. For that reason, many people confuse the two. Some objections to the practice of polyamory--for example, objections based on the perception that polyamorous relationships are inherently disempowering to women--arise from the misperception that polyamory or polygamy is the same thing as polygyny.

POLYGYNY: (Literally, poly many + gynos woman) The state or practice of having multiple wedded wives at the same time. Contrast monogamy; See related polygamy, polyandry, bigamy. Commentary: According to some sociologists, polygynous societies represent the most common form of society, with 850 of the 1170 societies recorded in Murdock's Ethnographic Atlas being polygynous. Modern Muslim societies are polygynous, and certain religious traditions, including Fundamentalist Mormonism (FLDS) in the United States, advocate polygyny.

POLYKOITY: (Literally, poly many + koitus, coitus sex) Anthropology The state or practice of having more than one sexual partner, either at the same time or over the course of one's lifetime, without regard to the relationship with those partners or their relationships with each other.

POLY/MONO; also, MONO/POLY: Colloquial Of or relating to a relationship between a person who self-identifies as polyamorous and a person who self-identifies as monogamous.

POLYSATURATED: Colloquial Polyamorous, but not currently open to new relationships or new partners because of the number of existing partners, or because of time constraints which might make new relationships difficult. Contrast polyunsaturated. Usage: Often considered humorous or slightly silly. Seems to be most common primarily in the western United States.

POLYSEXUAL: Colloquial Of or related to relationships which are sexually non-monogamous but which are not emotionally intimate. Usage: Sometimes condescending or derogatory; as Bill is not really polyamorous, but only polysexual. May indicate dismissal or derision of the relationship so named. See related swinging.

POLYTROTHISM: The state or practice of maintaining multiple egalitarian relationships, each of which is equal with respect to decision-making and other practical matters. Black Panther Party Central Committee member

Simba Wiley Roberts called it ultra-egalitarianism. Contrast primary/secondary; See related democratic family.

POLYUNSATURATED: Colloquial Polyamorous, and currently seeking or open to new partners. Contrast polysaturated. Usage: Often considered humorous or slightly silly. Seems to be most common primarily in the western United States.

POLYWOG: Colloquial, often humorous A child in a polyamorous household.

PRIMARY/SECONDARY: A polyamorous relationship structure in which a person has multiple partners who are not equal to one another in terms of interconnection, emotional intensity, intertwinement in practical or financial matters, or power within the relationship. A person in a primary/secondary relationship may have one (or occasionally, more than one) primary partner and one or more additional secondary or tertiary partners. A primary/secondary relationship may be "prescriptive" (that is, a primary couple consciously and deliberately creates a set of rules whereby any additional partners are secondary, often because this is seen as a mechanism which will protect the existing relationship from harm caused by additional relationships) or it may be "descriptive," and emerge from the nature and the situation of the relationship. See related tertiary, veto. Commentary: In practice, prescriptive primary/secondary relationships may create an environment where the people in those additional relationships feel unappreciated or insignificant, which is why some experienced polyamorous people do not construct their relationships along enforced primary/secondary lines.

PRIMARY: In a primary/secondary relationship, the person (or persons) in the relationship with the highest degree of involvement or entanglement, or sometimes the person accorded the most importance. A person may be primary either as a natural consequence of the circumstance and nature of the relationship (because that person has the greatest degree of financial entanglement, for example), or as a deliberate consequence of the relationship structure and agreements (as in the case of an existing couple who set out to add additional partners only on the condition that those existing partners are seen as "less important" than the couple). See also co-primary; Contrast secondary, tertiary. Commentary: People who deliberately seek to construct a relationship along prescriptive primary/secondary lines typically designate one and only one relationship as the primary relationship. People who do not seek to construct a relationship along prescriptive primary/secondary lines may have more than one primary relationship; a relationship becomes primary when it reaches a certain point of emotional commitment, practical entanglement, or both.

PUPPY-PILE POLY: Colloquial Polyamorous relationships in which all the people involved are to some degree physically and/or romantically involved with one another, with the implication that the people involved may share sex and/or sleeping space (hence, "all in one puppy pile").

QUAD: A polyamorous relationship involving four people, each of whom may or may not be sexually and emotionally involved with all the other members. See related N.Commentary: One of the most common ways for a quad to form is when two polyamorous couples begin romantic relationships cross-couple.

QUADOSHKA: See tantra.

RELATIONSHIP ANARCHY: A philosophy or practice in which people are seen as free to engage in any relationships they choose, that spontaneity and freedom are desirable and necessary traits in healthy relationships, that no relationship should be entered into or restricted from a sense of duty or obligation, that any relationship choice is (or should be) allowable, and in which there is not necessarily a clear distinction between "partner" and "non-partner." Relationship Anarchy is extending the tenets of Anarchy into relationships. It is fundamentally political in a way that more or less precludes the common social meaning of polyamory. If your focus is your relationship to social hierarchy, it is unlikely you are an Anarchist. - Carlos del Rio

RELATIONSHIP ESCALATOR: Relationships that are riding the traditional Escalator meet (or have a goal of meeting) all of these criteria — some more stringently than others. People can step off the Escalator by choosing to diverge from any of these criteria (or several at once).

1. Sexual and romantic exclusivity between two — and only two — partners. (Commonly called monogamy.)

2. Merging life infrastructure and identity. Sharing a home and other resources, such as finances. Also identifying strongly as a couple or family — perhaps to the extent that the individual identities of partners start to be eclipsed.

3. Hierarchy. Some relationships are considered more important than others, and thus "win" by default in many situations. On the Escalator, since you're allowed only one sexual/romantic partner, that relationship is considered more important than almost every other relationship (such as friendships), with the possible exception of parenting. (Off the Escalator, especially in ethically nonmonogamous relationships, hierarchy can get more complicated.)

4. Sexual connection, at least at the beginning of the relationship. (Sex often fades or disappears, especially in long-term monogamy.)

5. Continuity and consistency. Escalator relationships aren't supposed to pause or step back to a less-merged state. Also, Escalator partners have defined roles as partners — they aren't supposed to shift between being lovers and platonic friends, for instance. (Well, this often does happen, but it's not widely acknowledged.) From: https://offescalator.com/what-escalator/

On August 18, 2018, in a thread on the topic, Vee Christina offered:

"Dating --> cohabitating --> marriage --> baby --> burial is NOT the only form of progress and commitment a relationship can take. It makes me sad that there are folks who can't imagine emotional bonds that grow without those particular external markers. It's awesome if the escalator works for you, but I also invite people not to speak on that which they do not understand. 📷

"The escalator analogy is fairly simple. Once you make a decision to step onto an escalator, the rest of the movement occurs in a default, linear, inexorable progression. If you want to get off the escalator midway, that is what takes enormous effort toovercome the forces of inertia which are, through external action, moving you up the escalator. And once you step onto the escalator, everyone around you will treat that as a clear signal that you want to end up at the place where the escalator stops.

"A non-escalator relationship is more like walking along winding and forking paths in a garden. Any movement that occurs is *always* the result of internal agency and choice. The deeper into the garden you go, the more complicated it may be to find the path back out. But there is no force that is externally pushing you forward, that you must then also overcome if you wish to pause where you are, or circle back to an earlier spot in the garden, or leave the garden entirely. Once you walk into a garden, that isn't typically treated, in and of itself, as an indication of where you want or expect to end up. Multiple options remain open and valid and don't count as a "failure" of the project you began when walking in.

"This is why you can even have non-escalator relationships that end up looking, externally, like escalator relationships. This isn't what mine looks like, but you could in principle have a relationship with cohabitation, marriage, shared bank accounts, children, etc., that is entirely non-escalator. The escalator is about HOW different forms of commitment happen, and the level of choice, freedom, flexibility, and agency along the way. That's all."

RELATIONSHIP ORIENTATION: A preference for sexual or loving relationships of a particular form; as, for example, a preference for relationships which are monogamous, for relationships which are polyfidelitous, for relationships which are polyamorous, and so forth. See related switch (Def. 1). Commentary: Just as some people feel that their sexual orientation is fluid and a matter of choice where other people feel that their sexual orientation is fixed and not subject to choice, so do some people feel that their relationship orientation is subject to choice whereas others feel their relationship orientation is not a matter of choice. It has been my observation that some people seem to be inherently monogamous, and can't be happy any other way; some people seem to be inherently polyamorous, and can't be happy any other way; and some people seem to be able, under the right circumstances and with the right partners, to be happy in a monogamous or a polyamorous relationship. (From the More Than Two glossary.)

RESPONSIBLE NON-MONOGAMY: Any relationship which is not sexually and/or emotionally exclusive by the explicit agreement and with the full knowledge of all the parties involved. Responsible non-monogamy can take several forms, the two most common of which are polyamory and swinging, and is distinct from cheating in that everyone involved knows about and agrees to the activity. Responsible non-monogamy often explicitly spells out the conditions under which it is permissible for one person to take on additional partners, and often includes some form of safer-sex agreement such as a condom contract as well. Contrast monogamy, closed marriage.

ROCK & ROLL, ALSO ROCK 'N' ROLL and other variants: Originally, in the American South as far back as the 1920s, the phrase meant 'have sex,' as in 'let's rock & roll' or 'let's rock'; or sex play. See: "Though many strive to hide their human libidinousness from themselves and each other, being a force of nature, it breaks through. Lots of uptight, proper Americans were scandalized by the way Elvis moved his hips when he sang "rock and roll." But how many realized what the phrase rock and roll meant? Cultural historian Michael Ventura, investigating the roots of African-American music, found that rock 'n' roll was a term that originated in the juke joints of the South. Long in use by the time Elvis appeared, Ventura explains the phrase "hadn't meant the name of a music, it meant 'to fuck.' 'Rock,' by itself, has pretty much meant that, in those circles, since the twenties at least." By the mid-1950s, when the phrase was becoming widely used in mainstream culture, Ventura says the disc jockeys "either didn't know what they were saying or were too sly to admit what they knew."
— Christopher Ryan, <u>Sex at Dawn: The Prehistoric Origins of Modern Sexuality</u>

SACRED SEXUALITY: See tantra.

SAFE-SEX CIRCLE: See condom contract.

SAPIOSEXUAL: sa·pi·o·sex·u·al/ ˌsāpēōˈsekSH(oō)əl/

1. adjective (of a person) finding intelligence sexually attractive or arousing."I met a PhD student from Germany who told me that he was sapiosexual."

2. noun a person who finds intelligence sexually attractive or arousing."I'm a sapiosexual and I like to talk."

SCHRÖDINGER PARTNER; also, SCHRÖDINGER SWEETIE: see ambigusweetie. Etymology: From the Schrödinger's Cat thought experiment in quantum physics, where a cat in a box with a quantum detector may be both alive and dead simultaneously. Usage: Often considered silly.

SECONDARY: In a primary/secondary relationship, the person (or persons) in the relationship who, either by intent or by circumstance, have a relationship which is given less in terms of time, energy and priority in a person's life than a primary relationship, and usually involves fewer ongoing commitments such as plans or financial/legal involvements. A secondary relationship may be secondary as a result of a conscious decision on the part of the primary partners, or simply as a result of circumstance or the natural development of the relationship. See related tertiary.

SAPIOSEXUAL: Colloquial Of or related to sexual attraction to people based on their intelligence.

SECONDARY SIGNIFICANT OTHER: Colloquial A romantic partner other than one's primary partner or spouse. Usage: Used almost completely within the context of primary/secondary relationships.

SERIAL MONOGAMY: A relationship pattern in which a person has only one sexual or romantic partner at a time, but has multiple sexual or romantic partners in a lifetime, and may change partners frequently. Arguably the most common form of relationship in the United States, serial monogamy is predicated on the idea that a person can love more than one other person romantically in a lifetime, but not at the same time. Contrast polyamory, polygamy, swinging; See related monogamy.

SIGNIFICANT OTHER: Colloquial A romantic partner. Usage: The term significant other is intended to be free of assumptions about the gender of that partner. See related other significant other.

SOFT SWINGER: A swinger who has sexual intercourse or engages in other sexual activity only with his or her partner, but may do so at a swing club, or in the presence of other swingers. Occasionally, soft swingers may engage in some limited form of sexual activities, often stopping short of sexual intercourse, with partners outside the existing relationship. Usage: Common in the swinging community, but uncommon in the polyamorous community. Contrast hard swinger.

SPICE: Colloquial The plural of spouse. Usage: often considered humorous.

SPOUSE: A person's partner by marriage.

SOLO POLYAMORY (SOLO POLY): Solo polyamory is a fluid category that covers a range of relationships, from the youthful "free agent" or recent divorcee, brief, no-strings-attached connections, to the seasoned "solo poly" who has deeply committed, intimate, and lasting relationships with one or more people. Some solo polys have relationships that they consider emotionally primary, but not primary in a logistical, rank, or rules-based sense, and others don't want the kinds of expectations and limitations that come with a primary romantic/sexual relationship. (from the article, Solo Polyamory, Singleish, Single & Poly, by Dr. Elisabeth A. Sheff) https://www.psychologytoday.com/blog/the-polyamorists-next-door/201310/solo-polyamory-singleish-single-poly

SORORAL POLYGYNY: A form of polygyny where a man marries two or more women who are sisters.

SSO (initialism): See secondary significant other.

SUBMISSIVE: See BDSM: «submissive».

SUNK-COST FALLACY: Reasoning that further investment is warranted on the fact that the resources already invested will be lost otherwise, not taking into consideration the overall losses involved in the further investment. See https://www.logicallyfallacious.com/tools/lp/Bo/LogicalFallacies/173/Sunk-Cost-Fallacy

SWINGING: Also referred to as swinger(s). Couples married or in an open relationship, who exchange sexual partners. From http://swingerlifestyle.com/category/swinger-online-dictionary See also friends-first swinging, closed swinging, closed-group swinging, swing club. Commentary: The common perception of swinging is that those who engage in this behavior have sex outside of their existing relationship purely for recreation, and that emotional bonds or emotional intimacy are specifically excluded. This is true in many cases. However, in practice swinging is much more nuanced, and people who self-identify as swingers can and sometimes do form close emotional relationships with their partners. Some people see swinging and polyamory as two ends of a continuum, different in degree of intent, focus, and emphasis on romantic and emotional relationships rather than different in kind.

SWITCH: 1. A term used in the fetish and BDSM communities as a person who can perform both dominant roles and submissive roles in sex play or sex games or intimate role playing. See Franklin's [BDSM page] for more information about fetish and BDSM. See BDSM: «switch». 2. Colloquial A person capable of being happy in either a monogamous or a polyamorous relationship. (Both definitions are from Joreth Innkeeper's polyamory terms site at http://theinnbetween.net/polyterms.html) See also, AMBIAMOROUS.

SWOLLY: Colloquial A person who identifies as both polyamorous and also as a swinger; that is, a person who has multiple simultaneous relationships and also enjoys recreational sex in a swinging context. Etymology: The term was coined by Ken Haslam of the Kinsey Institute.

SYSTEMIC TRAUMA: Contextual features of environments and institutions that give rise to trauma, maintain it, and impact post-traumatic responses-provides a framework for considering the full range of traumatic phenomena. (Reference: https://www.ncbi.nlm.nih.gov/pubmed/24617751). Ron Young, founder of Black & Poly, explains its applicability to black and other oppressed communities being "...very unique to us. Some folks suffer from so much systemic trauma that it makes it virtually impossible to be in a Polyamorous relationship. The system has rattled them around in such a way that love of any kind is a struggle. (T)heir anger is projected on the folks closest to them because they can't get to the folks that really did them harm."

TARZAN COMPLEX: A behavior by outsiders – those not indigenous to the Black community – who alight from the carriage defining our conventions, critiquing our mores, and restructuring our social systems, who command all of our resources and allegiance and show us 'the way,' while we trip over ourselves trying to untangle the mysteries of the lives we have lived since time began. Ref: Espoused during an interview with Stokely Carmichael (Kwame Toure), leader of SNCC, the Student Non-violent Coordinating Committee, who also said: The first need of a free people is to define their own terms.

Also: Part of the canon of the Black Congress, Los Angeles, 1960s, an organization comprised of revolutionary nationalist and cultural nationalist organizations, the largest of which were the Black Panther Party and Ron Karenga's US Organization (Ron Karenga was co-creator of Kwanza). Both the Black Panther Party and the US Organization maintained collectives – communal living spaces – that championed open-relating styles that were dissimilar in principle, but both were patriarchal.

Also: From 'She Who Faces The Sun' at http://barefootandgolden.tumblr.com/post/92667470669/the-tarzan-complex-aka-superiority-complex: "Tarzan, described as a white man in many books and shows, also held the title of "King of the Jungle." He resolved conflicts of the apes and animals and was Christ-like in his guidance (of the indigenous Africans). Avatar, District 9, Step Up, and Game of Thrones all depict white characters going in the "wild" of a minority area and becoming as like them, with elevated status and leading them. White people found outside of their element are considered more accomplished, by the masses, than black people within theirs."

TERTIARY: A person (or persons) in a relationship which is generally quite casual, expects little in the way of emotional or practical support, or is very limited with respect to time, energy, or priority in the lives of the people involved. Contrast primary; See related primary/secondary, secondary. Commentary: A tertiaryrelationship may be very limited in scope or priority for many reasons, one of the most common of which is often distance.

TOXIC MASCULINITY: Toxic masculinity is a narrow and repressive description of manhood, designating manhood as defined by violence, sex, status and aggression. It's the cultural ideal of manliness, where strength is everything while emotions are a weakness; where sex and brutality are yardsticks by which men are measured, while supposedly "feminine" traits—which can range from emotional vulnerability to simply not being hypersexual—are the means by which your status as "man" can be taken away. - The Good Men Project. And: https://www.tolerance.org/magazine/what-we-mean-when-we-say-toxic-masculinity?fbclid=IwAR1Ne18jt5XJLa6lEJXuc0_BuGMDtNrmL0tOHrEpt9Mwnh_OB179CVSxkHU

TRIAD: 1. A polyamorous relationship composed of three people. 2. A union or group of three. Usage: In the sense of Def. 1, generally, the word triad is most often applied to a relationship in which each of the three people is sexually and emotionally involved with all the other members of the triad, as may be the case in a triad consisting of one man and two bisexual women or one woman and two bisexual men; however, it is sometimes also applied to vee relationships. See also flexuous triad.

TRIBE: A social division consisting of individuals, families, pods, or communities linked by social, economic, religious, or blood ties, with a common culture and dialect, typically having a recognized leader. A human social group.

TROIKA: A group marriage involving exactly three people. See related triad.

TROILISM: Sexual activity involving exactly three people; either in the form of three people simultaneously engaging in sexual activity, or in the form of one person watching while two others have sex. See related ménage à trois (Def. 1).

TROUPLE: see triad. Etymology: A neologism coined by combining "couple" and "triple."

TRUTH-TRIGGERED: an emotional, often subconscious reaction evident when the mere thought of telling the truth in unsafe environments triggers extreme fear, which stems mostly from childhood or spousal abuse, and/or past experiences of trauma, where being truthful resulted in swift and harsh punishment. Coined by Ron Young, founder of Black & Poly, in explaining that telling lies developed as a survival tactic in marginalized communities.

UNICORN: Colloquial; see hot bi babe. Usage: In dominant polyamory culture, almost always used of a hypothetical woman who is willing to date both members of an existing couple, agree not to have any relationships other than the ones with the couple, agree not to be sexually involved with one member of the couple unless the other member of the couple is also there, and/or agree to move in with the couple. So named because people willing to agree to such arrangements are vanishingly rare, whereas couples looking for a woman who will agree to these terms are incredibly common (The Innkeeper, MoreThanTwo.com, Bhramari Dasi's blog). There is no objective evidence to suggest that any of that is true, however (and see: https://www.facebook.com/notes/polyamory-loving-with-an-open-hand/the-myth-and-misconception-of-the-polyamorous-unicorn/330603197382812/). Whether a unicorn must be a woman depends on whom you ask and on what conversation you enter. In some communes (intentional communities), a single woman, with or without children, is called a unicorn. (Notation: in patriarchal swinging circles, a unicorn is, typically, a bisexual female who seeks male/female couples for sex play at swinger parties and privately, choosing to be with both simultaneously (MFF), but beholden to neither as it relates to romantic or sexual fidelity (done and gone, as it were). Source: SpecialKs on swinglifestyle.com)

VANILLA: A vanilla relationship is one that most closely mirrors the perceived relationship style of the dominant culture or community. In BDSM, for example, a vanilla relationship might be one that lacks a master/slave dynamic (https://www.librarything.com/topic/23531); in kink, it might be one that is essentially missionary. In polyamory, vanilla could mean monoamorous, for example. Whether a thing is vanilla is a matter of perspective; it is where you sit within concentric circles. The circles with greater radii are seen as dominant over those with smaller radii. Some references: https://poly.land/tag/vanilla-polyamory/ www.polyamory.com › ... › Polyamory › Poly Relationships Corner https://www.psychologytoday.com/us/blog/.../is-polyamory-form-sexual-orientation thestir.cafemom.com/love/184183/polyamory_101_what_the_curious

VASOPRESSIN: A hormone produced by the hypothalamus and released by the pituitary gland. Vasopressin is known to be involved in the regulation of blood pressure and the uptake of water by the kidneys, and is also believed to be involved in mediating such responses as aggression and mating. Levels of vasopressin in the body rise sharply immediately after sex; it is believed that this may play a role in new relationship energy. See related oxytocin.

VEE: Colloquial A polyamorous relationship involving three people, in which one person is romantically or sexually involved with two partners who are not romantically or sexually involved with each other. See also triad, pivot; See related quad, N.

VETO: A relationship agreement, most common in prescriptive primary/secondary relationships, which gives one person the power to end another person's additional relationships, or in some cases to disallow some specific activity, such as some specific sexual or «BDSM»-related activity. A veto may be absolute, in which one partner may reject another partner's additional relationships unconditionally, or may be conditional and used more as a way to indicate a serious problem in a relationship. Commentary: Not all polyamorous recognize or permit veto power. Veto is most common in primary/secondary relationship configurations, particularly in relationship configurations where an established couple is seeking additional partners. Veto is typically limited only to the primary partners, and a relationship which grants a veto power to a secondary partner is rare in the extreme.

WHITESPLAIN: A combining form of white and explain that means to explain something, particularly racism or racial dynamics, to a person of color from a perspective of white privilege and condescension. Reference: https://slangit.com/meaning/whitesplain

WOMANISM, WOMANIST: From Alice Walker's Definition of a "Womanist" from In Search of Our Mothers' Gardens: Womanist Prose Copyright 1983.

> 1. From womanish. (Opp. of "girlish," i.e. frivolous, irresponsible, not serious.) A black feminist or feminist of color. From the black folk expression of mothers to female children, "you acting womanish," i.e., like a woman. Usually referring to outrageous, audacious, courageous or willful behavior. Wanting to know more and in greater depth than is considered "good" for one. Interested in grown up doings. Acting grown up. Being grown up. Interchangeable with another black folk expression: "You trying to be grown." Responsible. In charge. Serious.

> 2. Also: A woman who loves other women, sexually and/or nonsexually. Appreciates and prefers women's culture, women's emotional flexibility (values tears as natural counterbalance of laughter), and women's strength. Sometimes loves individual men, sexually and/or nonsexually. Committed to survival and wholeness of entire people, male and female. Not a separatist, except periodically, for health. Traditionally a universalist, as in: "Mama, why are we brown, pink, and yellow, and our cousins are white, beige and black?" Ans. "Well, you know the colored race is just like a flower garden, with every color flower represented." Traditionally

capable, as in: "Mama, I'm walking to Canada and I'm taking you and a bunch of other slaves with me." Reply: "It wouldn't be the first time."

3. Loves music. Loves dance. Loves the moon. Loves the Spirit. Loves love and food and roundness. Loves struggle. Loves the Folk. Loves herself. Regardless.

4. Womanist is to feminist as purple is to lavender

RESOURCES

The main questions I had when I began my ENM journey was why would you do this? How would you do this? Where would you do this and with whom do you do this? Who can I talk to about my experiences…doing this? Below are a few resources that I believe can answer some of these questions. There are also sex experts/educators listed as a resource for those wanting to expand that area of their lives. Resorts and events where ethical non-monogamous relationships are welcomed so you may travel with all of your partners and enjoy the world together. Of course, additional books.

Coaching / Therapy / Education

1. Taylor K. Sparks

   OrganicLoven.com

   Sex and Relationship Coaching

   Organic Intimate Body Products

   taylor@organicloven.com

   866-978-2111

   IG: @organicloven, @sistersofsexuality

2. Parish Michelle Blair, Sex Goddess, Energy Consultant

    Parishblairtv.gumroad.com

    IG: @officialsexyspirittv

3. Ashley Cobb, Millennial Sex Educator

    sexwithashley.com

    ashley@sexwithashley.com

    IG: @sexwithashley

4. Chanel Jaali, Sex Educator, HIV/AIDS Activist

    jaalico.com

    jaali.company@gmail.com

    IG: @jaali_co

5. N. Jasmine Johnson-Decosta, Psychotherapist, Sex Educator

    BluePearlTherapy.org

    A solution-focused therapist who emphasizes a strength-based

    approach.

    IG: @bluepearltherapyllc

    813-419-2980

6. Kristopher Lovestone, Relationship counselor, Sex Educator, Author

    Consciouscock.com

    904-297-8657

    IG: @consciouscock

7. Erica Merrill, Therapist

    ElevatedWellnessCounseling.com

    elevatedwellnesscounseling@gmail.com

    980-430-0205

8. Renelle Nelson

    Marriage/Family Therapist, Sex Therapist

    AffairAfterCare.com

    Kaleidoscopeservicesllc.org

    Info@kaleidoscopeservicesllc.org

    480-800-2527

    IG: @noirsxtherapist

9. Perle Noire, Transformative Coach, Healing Through Seduction

    Blackburlesquequeen.com

    perlenoire@blackburlesquequeen.com

    IG: @theperlenoire

10. Evita Sawyers, Aka Evita Lavitaloca

    Personal Relationship Coach Specializing in Relationship Dynamics
    and Non-Monogamy

    214-490-5162

    IG: @lavitaloca34

11. Kenya K. and Carl Stevens, Relationship Experts, Love Coaches

    ProgressiveLoveAcademy.com

    IG: @progressive_love_academy

12. Krystal Taylor, Tantric Yoga

    www.krystaltantricyogi.com

    IG: @krystaltantricyogi

13. Charlie and Arienne Williams, Psychotherapist, Sex Educators

    SexBecause.com

    Specializing in PTSD, Sexual Trauma, Adolescent and Family

    Therapy, Couples Therapy

    1-888-6BECAUSE

    IG: @sexbecause

14. Coaches Nazir, Fatimah and Nyla, Polygymous Relationship

    Coaches, Educators

    Outstandingpersonalrelationships.com

    IG: @outstandingrelationships

    support@outstandingpersonalrelationships.com

Community - Polyamorous, Swinging, Sex-positive

1. Blackandpoly.org Ron Young, Founder

2. Tickle.life, Shakun Sethi, Founder

3. Feeld.com

4. Kasadie.com

5. LifestyleLounge.com

6. SDC.com

7. Swinglifestyle.com

Travel - Cruises, Resorts, Conferences

My company OrganicLoven.com offers a variety of adults only cruises, resorts and conferences throughout the year and the world! Visit my site and email me (taylor@organicloven.com) with any questions regarding the resorts, event producers, hotel takeovers.

1. Organicloven.com/sexy-getaways-adults-organic-loven

Books - Although there are not many books on ethical non-monogamy from an African-American perspective, I have found the books below helpful.

1. Designer Relationships: A Guide to Happy Monogamy, Positive Polyamory, and Optimistic Open Relationships, by Mark A. Michaels, Lyssa Browne, et al.

2. It's Called "Polyamory": Coming Out About Your Nonmonogamous Relationships by Tamara Pincus and Rebecca Hiles

3. Jealousy Survival Guide: How to Feel Safe, Happy and Secure in an Open Relationship, by Kitty Chambliss

4. Love's Not Color Blind: Race and Representation in Polyamorous and Other Alternative Communities, by Kevin A. Patterson and Ruby Bouie Johnson

5. Men's Polygamy Road Map, by Coach Nazir

6. More Than Two: A Practical Guide to Ethical Polyamory by Franklin Veaux, Eve Rickert, et al.

7. Opening Up: A Guide to Creating and Sustaining Open Relationships, by Tristan Taormino

8. Polysecure: Attachment, Trauma and Consensual Nonmonogamy by Jessica Fern, Eve Rickert, et al.

9. The Polyamory Breakup Book: Causes, Prevention, and Survival by Kathy Labriola, Leanne Yau, et al.

10. The State of Affairs, Rethinking Infidelity by Esther Perel

11. When Someone You Love Is Polyamorous: Understanding Poly People and Relationships, by Dr. Elisabeth Sheff

12. Women's Polygamy Roadmad, by Coaches Fatimah and Nyla

Endnote Resources

1.   Alex Gendler – YouTube

2.   Some believe the practice was widely known among specific subgroupsof British Roma, especially the Northumbrians. Parry, "Holy Land of Matrimony," 86; Tyler Parry, "married in Slavery Time: Jumping the Broom in Atlantic Perspective," Journal of Southern History 81 no 2 (2015): 281-284: Patrick O'Neil, "Bosses and Broomsticks: Ritual and Authority in Antebellum Slave Weddings," Journal of Southern History 75, no 1 (2009); 39-40. See also Alan Dundes, "Jumping the Broom': On Origin and Meaning of an African American Wedding Custom," Journal of American Folklore 109, no 433 (1996): 324-329; and C.W. Sullivan III, "Jumping the Broom;: A Further Consideration of the Origina of an African American Wedding Custom," Journal of American Folklore 110, no 436 (1997) 203-204.

3.   Ref Catherine Adams and Elizabeth Pleck, Love of Freedom: Black Women in Colonial and Revolutionary New England (New York: Oxford University press, 2010), 6-7.

4.   Lenhardt, "Marriage as Black Citizenship?," 1329 (see also 1327-1328, 1340-1341), http://ir.lawnet.fordman.edu/faculty_scholarship/655. See also Farmer-Kaiser, Freedwomen and the Freedmen's Bureau.

5.   Black Women, Black Love: America's War On African-American Marriage, (Seal Press, Oct 2020) Dianne M. Stewart.

6.   Black Females Sexual Myths: Impact on Swingers Culture; Valerie Poppel; International Book Market Service; 2020.

7.   The State of Affairs: Rethinking Infidelity, Esther Perel, Harper, Oct 2017

8.   www.polygamyeducation.com

9.   Jealousy Survival Guide, Kitty Chamblis, CreateSpace Independent Publishing Platform (October 31, 2017)